# Lay Preaching Basics

## *A Practical Guide to Leading Worship*

# Rosalie Sugrue

Philip
Garside
Publishing Ltd.

*Acknowledgements*
Thanks to Rev Dr Lynne Wall for her input on the gospel writers, and to
Philip Garside for his insights as an experienced lay preacher.

The author and publisher also gratefully acknowledge
the financial support of the Methodist Church of New Zealand


Print-on-demand edition
ISBN 978-1-722050-80-1


Philip Garside Publishing Ltd
PO Box 17160
Wellington 6147
New Zealand
books@pgpl.co.nz — www.pgpl.co.nz


eBook editions also available

# Contents

# Introduction

In these times of aging congregations, an increasing number of parishes are becoming unable to support a full-time presbyter and untrained lay people are finding themselves being shoulder-tapped to lead services. Volunteers are the salt of the earth, but all volunteers need some helpful pointers to be of use, regardless of the task.

Leading a service is a serious responsibility. Ideally all worship leaders should undergo a comprehensive course in Bible study, church history, theology (study of God: Greek *theos* "God" and *logos* "reason"), Christian beliefs (faith and practice), homiletics (the art of preaching), and other religions.

Potential worship leaders deserve to be mentored into accepting increasing worship responsibilities before contemplating leading an entire service. But we often find ourselves in situations far less than ideal. The intention of this book is to consider practicalities and set out the basics of worship leading, as well as providing some essential background knowledge, samples and resources.

# 1 — Help! The Preacher hasn't arrived

Don't panic. This can happen to any congregation at any time. When it does happen, a lay person on duty as a steward or door person, will slowly realise someone has to do something. That lay person may be you.

If the service sheets or PowerPoint are there, ready to use, your basic service is prepared. If this week's service sheet hasn't arrived, you may be able to find an old one you can use. Remember some Christian traditions have the same prayers every week. (If your congregation is of that ilk, use the prayer book, noting any specific instructions for laypeople.) If not using a set liturgy do a skim read through the material you have before starting the service. Where headings have no content following them you will have to wing it.

If no service sheet is to hand, use the hymnbook. Hymnbooks usually have some prayers somewhere. If yours doesn't, remind yourself that hymns are prayers set to music. Verses can be read as prayers.

If a children's time is expected grab a picture book from the kids' corner to read at the appropriate time. Check there are drawing materials available, so the children can draw something from the story to show the congregation at the end of the service.

Begin the service with a short explanation and a prayer, of this kind...

> O God, we don't know why _____ has not arrived but we ask that whatever has happened, you be with __ bringing your calming power to his/her situation, and also to ours as we continue our worship in this place. Amen.

Progress with:

- **Welcome and notices**
- **Call to worship:** If none provided, use the verse of hymn.
- **1st Hymn:** If no hymn indicated, invite suggestions from Praise section of hymnbook. Check that the organist/pianist is OK with the choice.
- **Prayer:** A 'gathering for worship' kind of prayer.

- **Family/Children's Time:** Read a story. Have the children suggest pictures to draw.

- **2nd Hymn:** A children's hymn. Even if no children are present, nostalgia is enjoyable.

- **Readings:** As already arranged, or a favourite passage of your choosing and say why you like this reading.

- **3rd Hymn:** Invite another favourite.

- **Sermon / Reflection Time:** "Today we will do our own reflection by sharing some of our faith thoughts..." Ask the people turn to neighbours for discussions between 2-3 persons.

These topics are suitable for any ordinary Sunday. Select one for the congregation to discuss:

- Three favourite hymns and why they are favourites?

- Why did you come here today? (Include your church history.)

- Three things you like about this church and three things that could be better.

- Three significant events in your faith journey.

- If it is a Special Sunday, suggest a topic based on the theme of the day, e.g. What does (Advent, Lent, Pentecost, Harvest Festival...) mean to you? Recall a particular (Advent, Lent...) that stands out as special to you.

- Conclude with general sharing: If a small congregation invite each pair in turn to say something; if large, invite anyone who wants to share something to speak.

- **Offering taken and blessed**

- **Pastoral Prayers – thinking of others:** Allow spaces for private prayer on matters of concern: international..., national..., local..., family and personal...

- **Lord's Prayer:** Conclude prayer time with all joining in.

- **Children show their drawings**

- **4th Hymn:** A well-known 'going out to be a Christian' sort of hymn.

- **Ending ritual:** Your usual: sung blessing, triple Amen, saying the Grace...

**Thank** everyone for helping.

**Enjoy** a well-deserved cuppa.

**Check up** on the missing preacher.

• • •

A good idea for any congregation, particularly those in a fragile position concerning regular worship leaders, is to compile your own A5 pew folder (that can be added to) that contains new hymns and prayers and basic liturgies.

If you feel led to become a regular lay worship leader there are a heap of basic things you need to know. Keep reading...

# 2 — Introduction to the Gospels

St Matthew    Gospel written c. 80–85 CE
              (Sources: Q, Mark and own material)

St Mark       Gospel written c. 65–75 CE
              (Sources: Q and own material)

St Luke       Gospel written c. 80–90 CE
              (Sources: Q, Mark, Matthew and own material)

              Note: The author of Luke also wrote, as a
              second volume, Acts of the Apostles.

St John       Gospel written c. 90–95 CE
              (Own material)

The Gospels can be considered as portraits of Jesus written from different perspectives to different audiences. Matthew, Mark and Luke are called the Synoptic Gospels because they contain similar material in some passages. The theory is they each had their own source and also drew from a common source that the scholars called Q. 'Q' comes from the German word *quelle* which means 'source'. John's Gospel is fundamentally different to the other three.

One of the most important developments in theology of recent times is the simple acknowledgement that Jesus was a Jew who lived at a particular time and place, and though exceptional in his understanding and relationship with God, was confined by his historical setting.

As a young person I learnt from the Penguin paperback *Verse and Worse* the rhyme: *How odd of God / To choose the Jews. But not so odd / As those who choose / A Jewish God / Yet spurn the Jews.* This notion has served me well, encouraging me into appreciating the historical Jesus and respecting the insights of postmodernism, that promotes the concept of no finite answers, but many faith possibilities to explore and many pluralities to value.

The Student Christian Movement and the SCM Press helped me appreciate what is known as 'higher Biblical criticism,' i.e. a close examination of the Biblical text that seeks to understand the literary composition, history and context of scripture. I believe any credible

21st century lay preacher must have a reasonable understanding of these discoveries.

## Matthew

Matthew, who was possibly a converted rabbi, writes from a Jewish perspective to what is thought to be a mixed Jewish and gentile Christian community. Matthew draws attention to the Jewish heritage of Christianity and even arranges his book in five discourses to reflect the five books of the Torah. He seeks enlightened continuity rather than a 'new faith.' With the motif of fulfilment, Matthew is careful to establish continuity between Israel and the church. More important than knowing the Torah is putting into action the will of God. Discipleship is a matter of obedience that reflects the love and compassion shown in the parables and in the concept of the Kingdom of Heaven established on earth. (Note that Matthew does not use the term 'Kingdom of God,' probably because Jewish people, a large part of his audience, do not name God directly.)

## Mark

Mark is the shortest and first written of the Gospels, (probably just after the destruction of Jerusalem in CE 70). It was once thought to be the memories of Peter written by a younger man sometimes identified as John-Mark, whose mother had a house in Jerusalem. It is now believed that he was a Gentile Christian as he lacks some Jewish understandings. Mark writes in short action-packed phrases that take the reader on a journey. Mark employs a literary device called the 'Messianic Secret,' that has Jesus saying to not tell anyone who he is. After the crucifixion a Roman centurion, significantly a gentile, reveals, "Truly this man was the son of God." Mark implies that the only way to understand Jesus is to follow him on a path of discipleship that will likely involve uncertainty and unavoidable suffering.

## Luke

Luke is viewed as an educated man, (perhaps a doctor), early historian and theologian, who interprets past events in the light of his understanding of who Jesus was. He is also the author of the Acts of the Apostles. Women feature more prominently in Luke's writing than in that of other New Testament writers. Christians should be communities marked by equality and respect where things are shared. Luke also uses the motif of a journey and presents Jesus as not only the Jewish Messiah but also 'a light to the gentiles.' His genealogy extends beyond Abraham to Adam, indicating the universal nature of salvation. Luke's preference is for readers to ponder for themselves the meaning of the parables and the journey. Although they live in hostile times, he reminds readers of the gift and power of the Holy Spirit. Joy is the natural response to that which was lost being found.

### John

John does not use material from the other Gospels, though he covers some events in common. John is particularly loved for the devotional content of his Gospel. It is a reflective composition that ponders the divine aspects of Jesus. It also contains more dialogue than the others, which gives us a feel for the characters. The number seven recurs with John recording seven miracles that he calls signs, seven discourses and seven 'I am' statements. Greek dualisms are used throughout: world/heaven, light/darkness, life/death, falsehood/truth, love/hate, and spirit/flesh. The setting is a hostile environment. The themes include the commandment to love, the Holy Spirit, unity, servanthood and self-offering. Once thought to be the Apostle, John is now known to be the last written gospel, which may have been authored by more than one person.

### Summary

To sum up, it has been said that the Synoptic Gospels present God information and John presents God experience. The Gospels were written during times of political upheaval and persecution. All seek to comfort and reassure their Christian communities. Each Gospel contributes something unique. All are important in presenting aspects that add to our understanding of who Jesus was, who he is for us and what God requires of us with the help of the Holy Spirit. The authors of the Gospels are revered as saints and officially known as the 'Four Evangelists.' History has many evangelists, (i.e. a Christian who persuades others to become Christians), but only the Gospel writers are given a capital E that denotes an official title.

## Gospel Symbols

Theologians and artists have delighted in making symbolic parallels and connections between various aspects of the Bible. Since the 5th century the Four Evangelists have been associated with the four 'living creatures' who surround the throne of God in Ezekiel 1:10 and Revelation 4:7.

|  | Matthew | Mark | Luke | John |
|---|---|---|---|---|
| **Apocalyptic Creature** | Winged human | Winged lion | Winged ox | Eagle |
| **Symbolises** | humanity, reason | royalty, courage | sacrifice, strength | heavens, Holy Spirit |
| **Theme of the Gospel** | Jesus is the Messiah, fulfilment | Son of God, authority, discipleship | Saviour for Jews and Gentiles | Jesus divine love, unity, servanthood |
| **Gospel Begins With** | Christ's genealogy from Abraham | John the Baptist roaring like lion in the wilderness | temple duties of Zechariah | Christ as Logos ('The Word') |

Matthew
Winged human

Mark
Winged lion

Luke
Winged ox

John
Eagle

# 3 — Essential Background Knowledge

## Basic Bible Concepts

### Old Testament Essentials

There is an academic preference for referring to the Old Testament as the Hebrew Scriptures or First Testament. While understanding the reasoning I find it easier in writing to use Old Testament and its abbreviation to OT. Also, being against all forms of discrimination, I am hesitant to support something that could feed into the concept of ageism!

The 39 books of the OT are an eclectic selection of writings that record the history and faith of the Hebrew people (later called Jews). These words were originally written on scrolls in Hebrew and take the form of many genres including poetry, parable and folk story, along with teachings and laws. None of it is history as we understand history.

In common with all ancient peoples, Jewish history was recorded in stories that were passed on orally, down many generations, before being recorded in written form. The Hebrew Scriptures place less importance on factual events than on what an event or story may mean in the history of its people. Within the first five books of the OT, several strands of oral tradition are placed alongside others that differ in describing the same incident.

Authorship, as in the New Testament, is sometimes ascribed to one person, when the work was actually written by an unknown person or, as is usually the case in the OT, many people. This was not done to deceive the reader. It was a cultural custom that connected the name of a well-known person with contents that were believed to endorse the attitudes of that person. This is similar to the way our advertisements use well-known people to endorse a product.

# A general Overview of OT content

| | |
|---|---|
| **Myths of Origin:** | Adam and Eve to Noah (Genesis chapters 1–11) |
| **The Patriarchs:** | Abraham, Isaac, Jacob and sons; tent dwellers (remainder of Genesis) |
| **Slavery in Egypt:** | Stories of Moses and the Egyptian plagues, crossing the Red Sea (Exodus) |
| **Wanderings in the Wilderness:** | (Exodus) |
| **The Ten Commandments:** | Developing the law (Exodus, Leviticus, Numbers, Deuteronomy) |

The above content is contained in the first five books known as the Pentateuch or Torah that the Bible calls the Books of Moses. These writings are particularly sacred to Jewish people.

| | |
|---|---|
| **Occupying the Promised Land:** | (Joshua) |
| **The Judges:** | Settlement with Judges as leaders (Judges). Includes stories of women and men. |
| **The United Kingdom:** | The reign of Kings Saul, David and Solomon. |
| **The building of the Temple in Jerusalem:** | By King Solomon. |
| **The Divided Kingdoms:** | Northern and Southern, also called Israel and Judah. |
| **The Exile:** | Both kingdoms were conquered with many of the people being taken to Babylon. |
| **The Return from Exile and Rebuilding of the Temple:** | The stories of the Kingdoms and the Exile are mostly told in 1 and 2 Samuel, 1 and 2 Kings and 1 and 2 Chronicles. |
| **The Writings:** | A mix of poetry, meditations, and historic fiction: Ruth, Esther, Job, Psalms, Proverbs, Ecclesiastes, Song of Solomon, Lamentations, and Daniel. |

**The Prophets:** Faith writings, some written before the Exile and some after, the major prophets being Isaiah and Jeremiah; the remainder of the OT books being the minor prophets.

### The Bible (in 70 words)

Here is a fun way to memorise the essential story:

> God made, Adam played, Noah sailed, Abram prevailed, Isaac bound, ram found, Jacob fooled, Joseph ruled, bush burned, Moses churned, Egyptians bled, Hebrews fled, sea divided, Law guided, Promise landed, Tribes banded, Judges appointed, Kings anointed, Psalms sounded, Wisdom expounded, Prophets warned, Exiled mourned, Jesus came, healed lame, Truth talked, Disciples walked, Christ died – then revived, Spirit flamed, Love claimed, Apostles preached, Gentiles reached, World changed, God remained.

### Things of interest

The book of Genesis details the saga of a wealthy family, the descendants of Terah.

Terah is thought of as the first recorded 'historic' figure. He had three sons and one named daughter. Abraham and Sarah (originally named Abram and Sarai) were half siblings as well as husband and wife. Sarah's maid, with Sarah's insistence, gave birth to Abraham's first son Ishmael. Sarah provided his heir Isaac. Much later Abraham acquired another wife who gave him many children.

Isaac and Rebekah were cousins; so was Jacob to the sisters Leah and Rachel.

The Abraham Saga does not follow the line of first sons. (See chart below.)

Jacob's sons: 1st wife Leah, gave Jacob 6 sons and 1 named daughter (Reuben, Simeon, Levi, Judah, Issachar, Zebulun and Dinah). Leah's maid Zilpah, provided 2 sons (Gad and Asher); as did Rachel's maid Bilhah, (Dan and Naphtali). Rachel had the 2 last sons (Joseph and Benjamin) and died in childbirth.

# Abraham's Family Tree

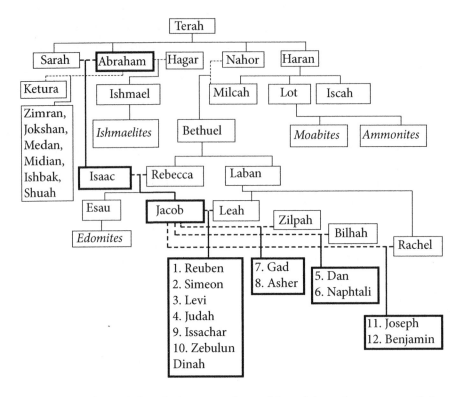

The sons of Jacob head the 12 tribes of Israel but the names of the actual tribes differ slightly in that the sons of Levi were designated as priests and were not allocated their own tribal land. Joseph's sons Manasseh and Ephraim were both allocated tribal land.

# More Bible Information

The word Bible comes from the Greek *biblia* meaning 'books' (as in bibliography).

The Protestant Bible contains 66 books (39 OT, 27 NT). The canon was finalised in AD 367.

The Holy Bible contains myth, poetry, laws, historic stories, gathered wisdom and teachings of a people seeking to understand the nature of God and what is required of them.

The OT was originally written in Hebrew. The NT was originally written in Greek. It is now believed that most of the OT was only written down during and after the return from Exile, many generations after many of the recorded events happened. The Hebrew scribes were influenced by some Babylonian stories.

## Documentary Hypothesis

This theory developed in the 18th and 19th centuries is widely accepted today. It suggests there are four main oral sources, known as J, E, D and P that form much of the Pentateuch.

- **J** uses Jahweh (Jehovah) or Yahweh for God (J and Y are interchangeable).

- **E** uses the name Elohim for God.

- **D** consists of Deuteronomy and similar material.

- **P** has a Priestly slant.

These sources had distinctive styles:

- **J** has simplicity and dignity, paints characters with bold strokes.

- **E** is systematic and detailed, lacking the vitality of J.

- **D** expresses ruthless monotheism as well as a personal God.

- **P** narratives and ritual laws – Creation is good, the medium of divine purpose.

*Timeline of main Old Testament Events*

| | |
|---|---|
| **The Patriarchs:**<br>c. 2000–1500 BCE<br>Abraham, Isaac, Jacob, Joseph | Genesis |
| **The Exodus:**<br>c. 1500–1300 BCE<br>Moses, slavery in Egypt and 40<br>years of wilderness wanderings | Exodus, Leviticus,<br>Numbers, Deuteronomy |
| **The Promised Land:**<br>1300–1020 BCE<br>Conquering and settling | Joshua, Judges |
| **The United Kingdom:**<br>1000 BCE<br>Kings – Saul, David and Solomon | 1 & 2 Samuel, 1 Kings,<br>1 & 2 Chronicles |
| **The Divided Kingdoms:**<br>922–597 BCE<br>Israel and Judah | 1 & 2 Kings, 1 & 2<br>Chronicles |
| **The Prophets:**<br>c.1050–686 BCE<br>King Saul to King Hezekiah.<br>Samuel, Nathan, Elijah, Elisha. | Isaiah, Hosea, Joel, Amos,<br>Obadiah, Jonah, Micah |
| 686–586 BCE<br>King Hezekiah to Exile | Nahum, Habakkuk,<br>Zephaniah, Jeremiah,<br>Ezekiel, Daniel* |
| **The Exile:**<br>686 – 586 BC<br>Many Jews forced to live in<br>Babylon. | Ezekiel, 2nd Isaiah |
| **The Return:**<br>539 BC –<br>Some Jews return from Exile. | Ezra, Nehemiah |
| 516 BCE<br>Temple rebuilt | Haggai, Zechariah, Malachi. |

* Some scholars now date Daniel in the 300s BCE.

There is a gap of about 500 years between the two Testaments with the most significant event being the occupation of Israel and Judah by Rome.

> **Note:** BC stands for Before Christ, but we now more frequently use BCE meaning Before Common Era. Common Era, CE, replaces AD, Latin for *Anno Domini* meaning 'the Year of our Lord' taken from the original phrase *'Anno Domini nostri Jesu...'*

## Bible Numbers

Lay preachers need to understand that numbers in the Bible are often used in a symbolic way and some have special meaning. When age is referred to in great numbers this is not meant to be taken literally. Adding years is a way of bestowing honour. 7, 3, 12 and 40 all have sacred significance.

**3** This numbers crops up as sacred in various places, culminating in the concept of the Trinity.

**7** The Jews gave the world the 7-day week that comes straight from the story of creation in the first chapter of the Bible and it reappears as a number of perfection.

**8** The '8th Day' being a day of blessing (1 Kings 8:66); day of infant circumcision. Adult baptism used the phrase the '8th day of creation' as symbolic of being a 'new creature' in Christ.

**12** Is a holy number as seen in the 12 Tribes and the 12 Apostles.

**40** Is interesting in that it is symbolic rather than literal. It has two meanings, one being 'perfection' as in the reign of David and other good kings and judges. But 40 can also mean a time of 'trial and testing' as in the days of the great flood, years in the wilderness, and days of the temptation of Jesus.

## A note about the Trinity

Throughout the Bible there is a recurring pattern of tri-unity that indicates three is a holy number. Other religions also recognise patterns of three as sacred.

However, the Holy Trinity that we honour as representing God is not detailed as such in the Bible. It wasn't considered as Christian doctrine until raised in 325, at the Council of Nicaea. The Bishops gathered at Nicaea adopted the Nicene Creed, which described Christ as, "God of God, Light of Light, very God of very God, begotten, not made, being of one substance with the Father." It took 50 more years of debating for the Trinity to become the orthodox doctrine of "three persons, one being." It is an attempt to explain the unexplainable. The Divine is a mystery, something humans feel and experience regardless of religion or culture.

> As I see it, humans do the best they can to make sense of things. God defies explanation, but the human relationship of parent and child is understood as a bond so special it transcends ordinary relationship to the realm of sacred. To expand sacred to divine requires an extra element. Many Christians make this connection through the Holy Spirit (or Holy Ghost as was a common name in former times). The Holy Spirit embodies the mystery of God's presence and is beautifully symbolised as wind being the breath of God, or 'Ruach' in Hebrew.

We tend to think of the Holy Trinity in masculine terms but 'Ruach' is grammatically feminine in Hebrew and is depicted as such in some early paintings of the Trinity. There are many lovely Trinity symbols to explore.

### Sorting out the Apostles

The Apostles are the 12 men chosen by Jesus to travel with him and be his special disciples. The Synoptic Gospels provide lists that are almost the same; The Gospel of John introduces Nathanael, thought to be Bartholomew, and Acts also contains a list.

The Twelve Apostles are harmonised as follows:

| Matthew 10:2–4 | Mark 3:14–19 | Luke 6:14–16 | Acts 1:13–14 |
| --- | --- | --- | --- |
| Simon Peter | Simon Peter | Simon Peter | Peter |
| Andrew | Andrew | Andrew | Andrew |
| James | James | James | James |
| John | John | John | John |
| Philip | Philip | Philip | Philip |
| Bartholomew | Bartholomew | Bartholomew | Bartholomew (Nathanael) |
| Thomas | Thomas | Thomas | Thomas |
| Matthew | Matthew | Matthew | Matthew |
| James (bar-Alphaeus) | James (bar-Alphaeus) | James (bar-Alphaeus) | James (bar-Alphaeus) |
| Thaddaeus | Thaddaeus | Judas (bar-James) | Judas (bar-James) |
| Simon | Simon | Simon | Simon |
| Judas Iscariot | Judas Iscariot | Judas Iscariot | Matthias (replaces Judas) |

Note: *bar* = 'son of' in Hebrew; *bat* = 'daughter of'; James bar-Alphaeus is also referred to in Mark's Gospel as 'James the less.'

These twelve men had a special relationship with Jesus, but it needs noting that Jesus had many other disciples or followers who at times journeyed with him. Of particular note are the women named in Luke 8:1–3:

> Soon afterwards he went on through cities and villages, proclaiming and bringing the good news of the kingdom of God. The twelve were with him, as well as some women who had been cured of evil spirits and infirmities: Mary, called Magdalene, from whom seven demons had gone out, and Joanna, the wife of Herod's steward Chuza, and Susanna, and many others, who provided for them out of their resources.

## Sorting out the Epistles of Paul

The Epistles are letters written to encourage groups or individuals at the very beginning of the Christian era. Although written before the Gospels they are placed in the second half of the New Testament between the books of Acts of Apostles and Revelation.

Traditionally 14 of these have been attributed to Paul and called the Pauline Epistles:

Romans – 1 & 2 Corinthians – Galatians – Ephesians – Philippians – Colossians – 1 & 2 Thessalonians – 1 and 2 Timothy – Titus – Philemon – Hebrews.

However, modern scholarship contests this and the current general consensus is that only the following seven letters were actually written by Paul:

Romans — 1 Corinthians — 2 Corinthians — Galatians — Philippians — 1 Thessalonians — Philemon.

It is thought that Paul may have influenced the content and some of the others. It is also suggested that he may have employed a secretary to write for him. The genuine Pauline Epistles are thought to have been written between 50 and 57 CE.

## Other Epistles

The book of Hebrews has long been considered to not match Paul's writing. The remaining Epistles: James – 1 and 2 Peter – 1, 2 and 3 John, and Jude, were traditionally attributed to the Apostles bearing their names. This is now considered unlikely but there are no firm theories on the authorship, other than they were early Christians who had been influenced by the teachings of the Apostles.

## Women of the Easter Story

Identifying the women is complicated as each Gospel records them differently and several of the women are called Mary. The name originates from the Old Testament, Miriam.

| Matthew | Mark | Luke | John |
|---------|------|------|------|
| **Women at the cross** | | | |
| many women ... who had followed Jesus from Galilee, ministering to him, among whom were Mary Magdalene and Mary the mother of James and Joseph and the mother of the sons of Zebedee (27:55–56) | women ... among whom were Mary Magdalene, and Mary the mother of James the younger and of Joses, and Salome (15:40) | the women who had followed him from Galilee (23:49) | his mother and his mother's sister, Mary the wife of Clopas, and Mary Magdalene (19:25) |
| **Women who accompanied the body to the tomb** | | | |
| Mary Magdalene and the other Mary were there, sitting opposite the tomb (27:61) | Mary Magdalene and Mary the mother of Joses saw where he was laid (15:47) | the women who had come with him from Galilee (23:55) | |
| **Women who went to the tomb after the Sabbath at dawn** | | | |
| Mary Magdalene and the other Mary 28:1 | Mary Magdalene and Mary the mother of James and Salome (16:1) | Mary Magdalene and Joanna and Mary the mother of James and the other women with them (24:10) | Mary Magdalene (20:2) |

### The Mary Dilemma

It is impossible to know for certain who was at the cross and tomb, or how many of them were named Mary. A surprising omission from the lists is Mary of Bethany, sister to Martha and Lazarus, who had a close relationship with Jesus. Some scholars conclude that Mary of Bethany and Mary Magdalene are one and the same. (Magdala not being her town of origin, but a title, 'magda' meaning 'great', i.e. the 'Great Mary').

There are also various other possibilities among the other women:

**Mary Magdalene:** Mary of Bethany?

**Mary of Nazareth:** Mother of Jesus, and though unlikely, could be the same person as...

**Mary mother of James and Joseph / Joses:** (and Jesus? – Matthew 13:55; Mark 6:3)

**The other Mary:** Possibly wife of Zebedee or **Mary wife of Clopas**. May be the unnamed disciple who lived at Emmaus, i.e. Mary wife of Cleopas?

Also named are:

**Joanna:** Wife of Chuza. She presents no other options and is named as a follower in Luke 8:3.

**Salome:** Sister of Mary and/or mother of Zebedee's sons? If so, this means James and John were Jesus' cousins, closer cousins than John the Baptist.

> **Note:** The only male disciple mentioned is referred to as 'the disciple whom Jesus loved' traditionally thought to be John (called John the Evangelist, as it was presumed he wrote the Gospel of John). It is now realised this was not possible. There is a theory that the beloved disciple may have been James, the brother of Jesus, taking a literal stance on 'Mother, behold your son.'

## Bible Men, Women and Children

*Men*

Take a guess, how many men are named in the Bible? The answer is a staggering 2,850. Well, what about women? Their total is considerably easier to add up, 160 is the approximation. It is impossible to be certain with the numbers because: there are different people with the same name; one person can be referred to by more than one name; and one name can have more than one spelling. But, what we can be sure of is there are over 3,000 individuals recorded in the Bible. Be amazed but don't despair, a good grasp of the main Bible characters is attainable! Less than 400 named persons are placed in situations that could be called 'their story.' The Bible contains many really great stories, along with some unfathomable incidents, but the vast majority of its people are males that only appear as names in long genealogies and lists of warriors or officials.

### Develop character confidence

Despite having listened to the Bible being read for decades most parishioners feel they can't name many Bible characters and shy off trying. Worship leaders need to have an understanding of the important characters. Try thinking your way through Genesis and jotting down names as you go, you will be surprised how they mount up. Move on to the Gospels thinking logically through the life of Jesus and you are likely to arrive at a decent total. Don't take up preaching until you can compile a decent list. A reasonable 'character aim' for beginner worship leaders is to name and a supply a fact for 100 Bible characters.

Bible word-searches and puzzles are excellent for expanding knowledge of Bible words and concepts. The Bible Challenge puzzles in the New Zealand Methodist Church's *Touchstone* relate to the Lectionary. The easiest way to get a handle on how the Bible story unfolds is via a well-illustrated children's Bible with a good index. Children's Bibles give the gist of the Bible story in sequence without getting side-tracked and usually do a good job of putting the important men into context. They seldom do justice to women. Make sure you can name and explain at least 20 females.

### Women

There are many Bible characters with interesting stories who are not given names. Various people are identified by location but there is a bias towards dropping female names in favour of identification by relationship, i.e. to a male relative or a location. Many Old Testament books including the Psalms and all the Prophets, do not name, or even mention women, an exception being the wife and daughter of Hosea. All the Bible books are presumed to be written by men, with the Book of Ruth the most likely exception.

In the Old Testament polygamy is widespread among wealthy families but gets no mention in the New Testament. Women are generally viewed as chattels, prided mostly for their ability to provide sons. But, there are significant exceptions in the OT, including Miriam, sister of Moses, the five daughters of Zelophehad, the Judge Deborah and prophetess Hulda. Various other women assume leadership roles and do daring things.

In the New Testament it is surprising how few women are noted as mothers. Mary and Elizabeth are given the only mother and infant stories. Although some women are given serving and passive roles, the majority of New Testament women are presented as strong individuals doing their own thing.

### Children

Stories involving children and youth are rare but get disproportionate attention through the abundance of picture books of Bible stories. Stay mindful that the Bible is adult literature. Bible stories packaged for children are sanitised and do not tell the whole story. Women in Bible times normally married young and most brides would have been girls in our eyes. There are also various stories of young men who may have been young teens.

## Important Bible characters

The following lists took years to compile and were completed before I had access to the Internet. These people are my selection of the most important characters of the Bible.

Those in *italics* have childhood/youth incidents referenced.

Women are in **bold** and referenced.

A few named women, who are not given stories, are included here as their names would not have been recorded without a reason. Unnamed women with important stories are also included.

*Old Testament*
**Genesis:**
Adam, **Eve** (3:20); Cain, Abel, Seth, Methuselah, Enoch, Noah, Shem, Ham, Japheth, Lamech, **Adah, Zillah** (4:19), Jabal, Juba, Tubal-Cain, **Naamah** (4:22); **Milkah, Ischah** (11:29); Abraham/Abram, Lot, **Lot's wife** and **2 daughters** (19:15); **Sarah/Sarai,** *Hagar* (16:1); *Ishmael, Isaac* (21:9); *Rebekah* (24:57–59); Esau, Jacob (25:22–27); **Keturah** (25:1); Laban, **Leah, Zilpah,** *Rachel,* Bilhah (30:1–9); **Dinah** (30:21); **Deborah** (35:8); **Mehetabel** (36:39) **Tamar** (38:6); *Perez, Zerah* (38:27–30); Potiphar, **Potiphar's wife** (39); Pharaoh, **Asenath** (41:50–52); Sons of Jacob: Reuben, Simeon, Levi, Judah, Zebulun, Issachar, Dan, Gad, Asher, Naphtali, *Joseph* (37); *Benjamin*; (42–43);[sons of Joseph] Manasseh, Ephraim; **Serah** (Genesis 46:17; Numbers 26:46).

**Exodus, Leviticus and Numbers:**
Pharaoh, **Shiphrah, Puah** (Exodus 1:15); *Moses* (Exodus 2:1–10); Jethro, **Zipporah** (Exodus 2:21); *Gershom* (Exodus 4:22–6), *Eliezer* (Exodus 18:2–7); **Jochebed,** (Exodus 6:20); Amram, **Elisheba** (Exodus 6:23); Aaron, *Miriam* (Exodus 2:3–9, 15:20); Balaam, Balak (Numbers 22:10); Zelophehad, **Mahlah, Noah, Hoglah,** *Milcah, Tirzah* (Numbers 26:33 & Joshua 17:3–6).

**Joshua and Judges:**
Joshua, Caleb, **Rahab** (Joshua 2:1); Othniel, **Achsah** (Joshua 15:17); **Jael** (Judges 4:17); Barak, Sisera, **Deborah,** Lappidoth (Judges 5:7); Jotham (Judges 6:7), Gideon, Jephthah, *Jephthah's daughter* (Judges 11:34), Manoah, **wife of Manoah,** Samson, **Delilah** (Judges 16:4).

**Of Royal connection:**
*Saul and his servant boy* (1 Samuel 9); **Merab,** *Michal* (1 Samuel 14:49–50); *David,* Jonathan, *Jonathan's arrow boy* (1 Samuel 20:35–39), **Rizpah** (2 Samuel 3:7); *Mephibosheth*; **Mephibosheth's nurse** (2 Samuel 4:4); *Mephibosheth's son* (2 Samuel 9:12) **Bathsheba** (2 Samuel 12:24); **Abigail, Tamar** (2 Samuel 13:1); Absalom (2 Samuel 15:1); **Abishag** (1 Kings 1:3); Ahab, **Jezebel** (1 Kings 16:31); Solomon, **Queen of Sheba,** Rehoboam, Jeroboam, **Wife of Jeroboam** (1 Kings 14:2); Jehoshaphat, **Azubah** (1 Kings 22:42); Nadab, Zimri, Omri, Asa, Ahab, **Queen Athaliah** (2 Kings 8:26); Joram, Jehu, **Jehosheba** (2 Kings 11:2–4), *Joash,* **Joash's nurse;** Uzziah, Jotham, Ahaz, Hezekiah, Amon, *Josiah,* **Jedidah** (2 Kings 22:1); **Hephzibah,** *Manasseh,* (2 Kings 21:1); Zedekiah (2 Kings 24.17).

**Others of the Kingdoms:**
Elkanah, **Hannah, Peninnah** (1 Samuel 1:2); *Samuel* (1 Samuel 2:18–21); Kish, Jesse (1 Samuel 11:20); Goliath, Joab, Gehazi, **medium / 'witch' of Endor** (1 Samuel 28:7); **two mothers of Solomon's kingdom** (1 Kings 3:16); **Widow of Zarephath** (1 Kings 17:10); *her son* (1 Kings 17:17–24);**Widow with oil,** *her children* (2 Kings 4:1); **Shunammite Woman** (2 Kings 4:8), *her son* (2 Kings 4:8-37); Naaman; *Hebrew maid* (2 Kings 5:2); **Gomer** (Hosea 1:3); **Asherah [Goddess]** (2 Kings 21:7); Priests: Eli, Oded (2 Chronicles 28:9); Prophets: Nathan, Elijah, Elisha, **Huldah [prophetess]** (2 Kings 22:14); **Noadiah [prophetess]** (Nehemiah 6:14); Isaiah, Jeremiah, Ezekiel, Hosea, Joel, Amos, Jonah, Micah.

**Characters from the Writings**
**Naomi, Orpah, Ruth** (Ruth 1:2–4); Boaz, Obed; King Lemuel, **Lemuel's mother** (Proverbs 31:1); Ahaserus, **Vashti** (Esther 1:9); **Esther** (Esther 2:7); Mordecai, Haman, **Zeresh** (Esther 5:10); Job, **Job's wife** (Job 2:9); Eliphaz, Bildad, Zophar (Job 2;11); **Jemimah, Keziah, Kerenhappuch** (Job 42:14); *Daniel, Shadrach, Meshach, Abednego* (Daniel 1:3–7); Nebuchadnezzar; Belshazzar; **Wife of Belshazzar** (Daniel 5:10–12); Darius (Daniel 5.31).

*New Testament*
**Gospels:**
Joseph, **Mary** (Matthew 1:18); *Jesus* (Matthew 1, Luke 1); *John the Baptist* (Luke 1, Matthew 3:1), Herod, **Herodias** (Matthew 14:3); Jairus, Bartimaeus, Zacchaeus, Barabbas, **Mary Magdalene, Mary mother of James & Joseph** (Matthew 27:56); **Salome** (Mark 15:40); Tiberius, Pilate, **Elizabeth** (Luke 1:36); **Anna** (Luke 2:36); **Joanna, Susanna** (Luke 8:3); **Mary, Martha** (John 11:1); Lazarus; **Mary wife of Clopas** (John 19:25); Nicodemus, Joseph of Arimathea, Cleopas. Apostles: Matthew, John, James, Andrew, Peter, Philip, James the less, Simon the Zealot, Judas son of James, Judas Iscariot, Thaddaeus, Philip, Thomas, Bartholomew/Nathanael, *naked young man* (Mark 14:51–2) [John Mark of Acts?].

**Un-named Gospel women:**
**Peter's mother-in-law** (Matthew 8:14); *Jairus' daughter* (Matthew 9:18); **Woman with haemorrhage** (Matthew 9;20); **Daughter of Herodias** (Matthew14:6); **wife of Zebedee** (Matthew 20:20); **Woman**

with **alabaster jar** (Matthew 26:7); **two Servant Girls** (Matthew 26:69–71); **Pilate's wife** (Matthew 27:19); **Sisters of Jesus** (Mark 3:32); **Syrophoenician Woman,** *her daughter* (Mark 7:26); **Woman with two coins** (Mark 12:42); **Widow of Nain** (Luke 7:11); **Woman in crowd** (Luke 11:27); **Crippled Woman** (Luke 13:11); **Companion of Cleopas** (Luke 24:18); **Woman of Samaria** (John 4:7); **Woman taken in adultery** (John 8:3).

Women in Parables:
**Baker** (Matthew 13:33); **Ten Bridesmaids** (Matthew 25:1); **Sweeper** (Luke 15:8); **Persistent Widow** (Luke 18:3).

Acts of the Apostles:
Peter, Saul / Paul, Ananias, Simon, Cornelius, Barnabas, Silas, Felix, Festus, Agrippa, Ananias, **Sapphira** (5:1); Philip, **Candace** (8:27); Peter, **Tabitha/Dorcas** (9:36); **Mary of Jerusalem,** John Mark (12:12); **Rhoda** (12:13); *Timothy* (16:1–3); **Lydia** (16:14); *Eutychus* (20:9), *Paul's nephew* (23:16–22); **Damaris** *(17:34);* Aquila, **Priscilla / Prisca** (18:2); Apollos (18:24); **Drusilla** (24:24); **Bernice** (25:13); **Artemis / Diana [Goddess]** (19:24), Gallio, Felix, Festus, Caesar, Claudius, Publius.

Women named in the Epistles:
**Phoebe** (Romans 16:1); **Mary** (Romans 16:6); **Junia** (Romans 16:7); **Tryphaena, Tryphosa,** Persis, (Romans 16:12); **Julia,** Olympas, (Romans 16:15); **Chloe** (1 Corintians 1:11); **Euodias / Euodia, Syntyche** (Philippians 4:2); **Nympha** (Colossians 4:15); Timothy, **Eunice, Lois** (2 Timothy 1:5); **Claudia** (2 Timothy 4:21); **Apphia** (Philemon 1:2).

# Lists of things (Animal, Vegetable, Mineral) mentioned in the Bible

Different versions of the Bible use different names for various things including, plants, animals and objects. I have compiled the following list as I find them interesting, and useful for preparing Bible puzzles and quizzes. For cafe style services they can be used for creating discussion starter 'table mats' or activity sheets for young people and adults. I haven't included many references because, when you know what to look for, it is now so easy to search online with Bible Gateway.

**KJV** indicates King James Version or Authorised Version; **GNB** Good News Version; the others are found in most versions. My version of choice is the **RSV**, Revised Standard Version, or the **NRSV**, New Revised Standard Version, as it makes an effort to be gender neutral where appropriate.

## Birds:
Bittern (KJV), buzzard, dove, chickens, chicks (GNB), cock, cormorant, crane, cuckow, eagle, hawk, night-hawk, hen, heron, falcon, fowl, kite, osprey, ostrich, owl, partridge, peacock, pelican, pigeon, quail, raven, seagull, sparrow, stork, swallow, swan (KJV), vulture, winged fowl.

## Mammals:
Antelope, ape, ass, badger, bat, bear, boar, bull, calf, camel, cattle, coney (KJV), rabbit GNB), cow, cubs, deer, doe, dog, donkey, ewe, ferret (KJV), fox, gazelle, goat, hare, hart, hedgehog, hind, horse, hyena, ibex, jackal, kid, lamb, leopard, lion, mole (KJV), mouse, mule, ox, pig, porcupine, rabbit, ram, roebuck, sheep, swine, weasel, wolf.

Surprising omissions: rats, found in most places; domestic cats, in Egypt in Bible times.

## Insects and creepy-crawlies:
Ant, cricket, flea, flies, frog, gnat, grasshopper, hornet, insect, lice, locust, moth, snail (KJV), scorpion, spider, worm, viper.

## Reptiles:
Adder, chameleon, crocodile, gecko, lizard, serpent, snake, tortoise (KJV), turtle.

## Fantasy creatures:
Cockatrice, dragon, Leviathan (sea-monster), satyr, seraphim, unicorn, Behemoth, hippopotamus (Job 40:15); Leviathan, crocodile (Job 41:1)

**Likely explanations for some KJV 'fantasy' creatures...**

Behemoth  (Job 40:15) may be a dinosaur skeleton – Tyrannosaurs Rex?

Cockatrice  (Jeremiah 8:17) basilisk (mythology kills with a glance); RSV venomous snake (cobra)

Dragon  (Isaiah 34:13) later OT translations usually substitute jackal

Leviathan  (Job 41:1) sea monster – a crocodile

Satyr  (Isaiah 13:21) the dog-faced baboon worshiped by the Egyptians

Sea monster  (Lamentations 4:3) that gives suck to its young, a whale

Seraphim  (Isaiah 6:2) angel of high rank characterised by six wings

Snail  (Psalm 58:8) thought to be a slug with an internal shell

Tortoise  (Leviticus 11) called great lizard in later versions

Turtle  (Song of Solomon 2:12) turtle-dove or pigeon

Unicorn  (Isaiah 34:7) later versions give wild ox or rhinoceros

**Trees:**

Acacia, algum (Grecian juniper), almond, apple (more likely apricot), ash, balm, balsam, box-tree, broom, cedar, chestnut, cypress, date, ebony, elm, fig, fir, gopher, hazel, hyssop, juniper, mulberry, mustard, myrrh, oak, palm, pine, poplar, pomegranate, sycamore, turpentine tree, walnut, willow

**Bushes and grasses:**

Bramble, 'burning bush' (possibly a bramble), buckthorn, bulrush, reeds, flax, thistle, thorn.

**Flowers:**

Almond blossom, crocus, hemlock, henna blossom, lily, lotus, myrtle, pomegranates, rose, rolling thing (rose of Jericho or resurrection flower), rose of Sharon (tulip).

Song of Solomon names the most flowers, e.g. rose, lily (2:1); henna blossom (1:14); pomegranates in bloom,

'Lilies of the field' implies wild flowers and are unlikely to be what we think of as lilies.

**Grain:**
Wheat, barley, corn, millet, spelt, rye.

Rye, written 'rie' (Exodus 9:32, KJV); translated as 'spelt' in later versions, e.g. 'And you, take wheat and barley, beans and lentils, millet and spelt, and put them into a single vessel, and make bread of them.' (Ezekiel 4:9). Corn is not named but various 'grain' translations are likely to be 'corn', e.g. Amos 8:5.

**Fruit and nuts:**
Apples ('apples of gold' may mean apricots), almonds, chestnuts, figs, grapes, pomegranate, mulberry, olives, pistachio nuts, raisins, walnut.

**Vegetables:**
Beans, cucumber, leeks, lentils, mandrakes, melons, onions.

**Herbs & Spices:**
Aloes, balm, bitter herbs (dandelion, endive, chicory, lettuce, sorrel), caraway, cassia, cinnamon, coriander, cumin, dill, frankincense, garlic, henna, hyssop, mint, myrrh, mustard, nard, rue, saffron, salt, spices.

**Meat:**
Fish, fowl, game, goat, lamb, calf.

**Drink:**
Milk, water, wine.

**Dairy & processed:**
Bread, butter (curds), cakes, cheese, flour, honey, loaves, milk, wine, eggs.

> Food lists, as gifts, occur in the Joseph and Abigail stories.

**Colours:**
Amber (Ezekiel 1:27); black, blue, brown, crimson, green, grey, golden, purple, red, ruddy, scarlet, white, yellow, vermilion (Jeremiah 22:14); 'many colours' – Joseph's coat, (KJV) – considered a mis-translation that should have been 'long sleeves' indicating the favourite son did not have to work.

**Colour Sayings:**
Black as soot; White as snow; Green pastures; Red in the morning shepherds' warning.

**Fabric:**
Cotton, leather, linen, sackcloth, silk, skins, wool.

**Boats:**
Noah's Ark ('gopher wood' could mean cypress or wood covered with pitch); raft (cypress and cedar), Jordan ferry; Jonah's journeys; apostles and Jesus (fishing trips and transport); Paul's journeys.

**Pleiades**
*Matariki* – Māori – New Zealand; also *Subaru* – Japan, Job 9:9; 38:31 and Amos 5:8

**Biblical Occupations:**
Baker, blacksmith, builder, butler, carpenter, carver, commander, cupbearer, doctor, doorkeeper, farmer (crop, grain, grapes, livestock), fisherman, governor, guard, hewers of wood, hunter, jailer, judge, king, labourer, maid, magistrate, mason, merchant, midwife, mother, musician, nurse, potter, priest, prophet, prostitute, queen, sailor, shepherd, slave, seamstress, sentries, servant, silversmith, smith, soldier, spy, stone-cutter, tanner, tax-collector, tentmaker, trader, wardrobe keeper, wife.

**Clothing:**
Aprons, ashes, breeches, cap, cloak, coat, cotton, crown, earrings, ephod, garment (seamless), grave-cloths, girdle, linen, loincloth, mitre, robe, swaddling-cloths, sandals, shoes, staff, tunic, turban, veil. Anklets, bracelets, earrings, nose-ring, rings.

**Cloth:**
Cotton, leather, linen, sackcloth, silk, skins, wool.

**Colours of cloth and cord:**
Purple, crimson (scarlet), blue, white.

**Fabric related:**
Binding, chequer-work, cloth, cut, embroidered, fringes, garments, hem, laced, loops, made, make, mending, needle, patch, pinned, plaited, pleated, purple, scarlet, seam, seamless, sewed, stripes, tacked, tucked, woven.

**Building related:**
Archway, axe, beam, booth, build, builder, built, cellars, ceiling, chimney, cistern, city, clay, corner-stone, courtyard, door, doorposts, dungeon, floor, foundations, foundation-stone, gates, house, kitchen, ladder, lattice, lintel, nails, palace, plumb-line, roof, room, stairs, steps, tabernacle, temple, tower, wall, well, windows.

**Utensils:**
Bowls, cauldron, cooking pots, cups, dishes, flagons, griddle, jars, jugs, pots, pen and ink, oven, plates, stove, water-jars; vessels of wood and stone; (KJV) 'cruse' small earthenware container for holding liquids.

**Furnishings:**
Altar, bed, bench, broom, candlestick, carpet, chair, curtains, seat, table, throne, articles of ivory, costly wood, bronze, iron, and marble; statues and images.

**Musical Instruments:**
Bells, castanets, cornet, cymbals, flute, harp, horn, lyre, pipe, psaltery (various harp type instruments), tambourines, shalishim (triangles), timbrel (drum), trumpet and choirs.

**Weapons:**
Arrow, axe, bow, club, dart, fire, javelin, jawbone, knife, lance (lancet), millstone, quiver, ram's-horn, spear, sling, staff, stone, sword, tent-peg.

**Metals and Precious Stones:**
Agate, amethyst, beryl, brass, bronze, carbuncle (emerald), copper, coral, crystal, diamond, emerald (garnet), glass, gold, iron, ivory, jacinth (sapphire), jasper (jade), lead, ligure (hyacinth), onyx, pearl, precious-stone, rubies, sapphires (lapis), sardius (sard), silver, steel, tin, topaz (chrysolite).

**Money:**
Shekels of silver, talents / pieces of silver and gold; gold coins, silver coins, copper coins.

# Examples of Jesus' teaching referring to common things

**Sermon on the Mount:**
Salt, light, lamp, city, hill, treasure, moth, rust, barns, food, drink, clothes/clothing, lilies, birds, pearls, swine, bread, stone, gate, wolves,

thorns, figs, thistles, trees, fruit, rock, rain, flood, winds, sand, hair, log, speck.

**In other teachings of Jesus:**
Bread, wine, water, birds, flowers, mustard seed, corn, vineyard, labourers, barns, wheat, figs, coins, sparrows, sheep, goats, weeds, net, fish, pearls, tower, money, sheep, leaven, wineskins.

## Teachings of Paul

### Fruits of the Spirit: Galatians 5:22–23
'But the fruit of the Spirit is: love, joy, peace, patience (forbearance or long-suffering), kindness, goodness, faithfulness, gentleness and self-control'

### Gifts of the Spirit: 1 Corinthians 12:8–10
Word of wisdom, word of knowledge (teaching) faith (faithfulness), gifts of healing, working of miracles, prophecy, discerning of spirits, speaking in tongues, interpretation of tongues.

## Common Expressions used in everyday speech with Biblical origins

*Compiled from:*
*'I Never Knew that was in the Bible' Edited by Martin H. Manser, 1999*

| | |
|---|---|
| Apple of the eye | Psalm 17:8 |
| Blind leading the blind | Matthew 15:14 |
| Bone of my bones and flesh of my flesh | Genesis 2:23 — creation |
| Born again | John 3:3 — Nicodemus |
| Bottomless pit | Revelations 11:7 — judgment |
| Can a leopard change its spots? | Jeremiah 13:23 — can't be changed |
| Cast pearls before swine | Matthew 7:6 — words of Jesus |
| Chosen few | Matthew 22:14 — words of Jesus |
| Count the cost | Luke 4:28 — cost of being a disciple |
| Cover a multitude of sins | 1 Peter 4:8 — charity |

| | |
|---|---|
| Days of one's life | Psalm 23:6 — as long as one lives |
| Drop in the bucket | Isaiah 40:15 — human insignificance |
| Eleventh hour | Matthew 20:1-16 — workers in the vineyard |
| Eye for an eye | Exodus 21:22; Matthew 5:38-39 |
| Fall from grace | Galatians 5:4 — lose privilege |
| Fat of the land | Genesis 45:18 — promise to Joseph's brothers |
| Fear and trembling | Philippians 2:12 — deep reverence |
| Feet of clay | Daniel 2:23 — hidden weakness |
| Fell on his sword | 1 Chronicles 10:4-5 — suicide or resignation |
| Filthy lucre | 1 Timothy 3:8 — greed for money |
| Fly in the ointment | Ecclesiastes 10:1 — spoiler |
| Forbidden fruit | Genesis 2:29 — Adam and Eve |
| Four corners of the earth | Isaiah 11:12 — Lord will gather Judah |
| God save the king | 1 Samuel 10:24 — people acclaim Saul as king |
| Golden rule | Matthew 7:12 — do unto others...) |
| Holier than thou | Isaiah 65:5 — describing a rebellious people |
| Kill the fatted calf | Luke 15:23 — lavish celebration |
| Leopard cannot change its spots | Jeremiah 13:23 |
| Measure for measure | Matthew 7:2 — fair judgment) |
| Nothing new under the sun | Ecclesiastes 1:9 |
| Old wives fables (tales) | 1 Timothy 4:7 |
| Offer an olive branch | Genesis 8:11 — dove returning to ark |
| Powers that be | Romans 13:1 |

| | |
|---|---|
| See the light | Acts 9:3 — Paul on Damascus Road |
| Sign of the times | Matthew 16:3 — red morning shepherds' warning |
| Skin of one's teeth | Job 19:20 |
| Spirit willing, flesh weak | Matthew 26:42 — warning to sleepy disciples |
| Suffer fools gladly | 2 Corinthians 11:19 |
| Sweat of thy brow | Genesis 3:19 — expulsion of Adam and Eve |
| Teeth set on edge | Jeremiah 31:29–30 |
| Thief in the night | 1 Thessalonians 5:23 |
| Things in common | Acts 2:44 — believers sharing possessions |
| Thorn in the flesh | 2 Corinthians 12:7 — Paul's personal problem |
| Time and place for everything | Ecclesiastes 3:1–8 |
| To the pure all things are pure | Titus 1:15 |
| Wheels within wheels | Ezekiel 1:16 |
| Writing on the wall | Daniel 5:12 — ominous sign |

# 4 — Making Reflections Memorable

Think back over your years as a pew-sitter. What church memories immediately come to mind? Was it the music and singing, the general atmosphere and how you felt, a particular incident, or were your first thoughts the words from sermons?

Hopefully you can remember some stirring, moving and challenging words delivered from pulpits and the Bible texts that invoked them. But speaking generally, most sermons go unremembered. A major reason for this is that listening is seldom as memorable as participating.

The music and words of hymns stay with the singers in the way a sermon never can. This is why it is so important to choose hymns with care. Hymns carry our theology. If you are stuck on hymns written in the 18th and 19th centuries that is where your theology will be. This not only does a disservice to your congregations, it harms you. Do you want to end up in a dementia unit with the words of your most used hymn as your only remembered faith statement?

Brilliant preachers can and do preach sermons with no aids other than words and pauses that are memorable and life changing. Lay worship leaders are seldom brilliant preachers. However, there are ways of making a reflection more memorable than if you had merely read words written as a religious essay. If you do view sermons as religious essays, the school classic 'What I did in the holidays' is likely to be more memorable than any reflection you ever write.

## Engaging Techniques

### Questions
Rhetorical questions are a standard component in sermons and they have a place in reflections, but questions that invite answers can be more meaningful. With small congregations there are times when I engage the whole congregation in a brief discussion. Regardless of size I ask the occasional questions direct to the congregation. My favourite question ploy to involve everyone is to have the congregation discuss two or three questions in pairs, usually at the beginning of a reflection. Conclusions may or may not be shared depending on

numbers and time. Questions for pairs need to be opinion based rather than knowledge (or lack of) based. The questions I began this section with may be good starter for you to use.

## Tangible Items

Pictures to reflect on: Paintings and photographs make wonderful aids for silent meditation or with background music, and can be displayed on PowerPoint, but are more useful printed on the service sheet. One picture can fill a page or put up to six smaller pictures on the same theme, e.g. famous paintings of a Bible story, pictures of Jesus, images that symbolise the Holy Spirit. Contemplate: What is this picture saying to me?; or with multiple pictures, which image speaks most clearly to me, and why?

With small congregations it is easy to prepare individual small items that convey a message, such as a flax woven cross, or a single pipe-cleaner folded into a cross shape that fits in a pocket; a shell to remind of the Pilgrim way, St James or the Wesley Coat of Arms; or provide paper slips or cardboard shapes for people to write a quotation or personal commitment on. These can be collected and blessed with the offering or taken home. Other take-home objects suitable for congregations of any size could include: a flower, fern, seed, nut, feather, or stone that remind of your message.

Some years ago, I preached a sermon that detailed Joshua crossing the river Jordon and building an altar of river stones. At the end of the sermon I had the steward hand out small river stones and concluded with these words: Take this stone and keep it in your pocket. When you feel it be prompted to think: God made this stone. God is good. This stone reminds me to be good. God was with Joshua and God is with me. This stone reminds of Gods faithfulness. Two years later when leading another service in this church, a man came to me during morning tea and presented me with the stone he had been carrying in his pocket. By now a well-travelled stone that he wanted to return. The man lived in Holland and has family here that he visits when he can.

## Other Voices

To relieve the monotony of my words during a reflection I like to employ other voices to read a pertinent poem or mediation; or

41

sometimes two people alternatively reading a selection of quotes, texts or facts.

I have also done various dialogues with my daughter that feel into Biblical characters. (These can be found in my *Sophia & Daughters*, now only available as an eBook.) Also in this book are monologues that can form part of a reflection. When I move into character mode in the pulpit I add a headdress, e.g. a tiara for Esther, coloured headscarves for ordinary women, striped tea-towels secured with a band of black elastic for men and crowns for kings.

I supplement or substitute a reflection with the occasional short play reading. (See Ten Plays: *Short, easy dramas for churches*)

### Active Participation by All
The following reflection activity would work for a cafe service, but I used it in the context of a formal service, with a congregation of about 20 adults. The concept could be adapted for various Bible characters.

My reflection centred on King David. After some introductory comments I said:

> Instead of me recounting the life of David, I thought
> it would be more rewarding for you to recall what you
> know about David and share your impressions of this
> man. To aid you this task I have prepared some questions
> to get you started. Form groups of 3–4 where you are.
> Share your thoughts and go with the best guesses.

Give a prepared doubled sided paper and pen to each group; allow about 5 minutes a side.

### Side 1:
Space the questions to fill the page:

*David – from Peasant Youth to Mighty King*

| | | |
|---|---|---|
| 1. | What was David's job as a youth? | 1 Samuel 16:11 |
| 2. | How do we know he was good at his job? | 1 Samuel 17:34-35 |
| 3. | Can you name his parents? | 1 Samuel 17:12 |
| 4. | Where did he come in his family? | 1 Samuel 16:11 |

| 5. | Why did young David go to the battle field? | 1 Samuel 17:17 |
| 6. | How did he kill Goliath? | 1 Samuel 17:48 |
| 7. | What was the prize? | 1 Samuel 17:25 |
| 8. | King Saul employed him as what? | 1 Samuel 16:21-23 |
| 9. | Why did he fall foul of Saul? | 1 Samuel 18:6-9 |
| 10. | Who was David's best friend? | 1 Samuel 18:3 |
| 11. | Name as many of his wives as you can. | 1 Chronicles 3:1-10 |
| 12. | Name some of his children. | 1 Chronicles 3:1-10 |
| 13. | Why did the prophet Nathan rebuke David? | 2 Samuel 12:9 |
| 14. | How long was David's reign? | 1 Kings 2:11 |
| 15. | Which son succeeded him? | 1 Kings 2:12 |
| 16. | What had David not achieved that he asked his son to do? | 1 Kings 5:2-5 |

**Side 2:**

Space the questions to fill the page – or go creative and draw a Star of David with 6 points and a centre to fill with words.

*David – from Peasant Youth to Mighty King*

**a. Describe David**

As you imagine him in relation to what you know about him.

- Appearance:
- Talents:
- Nature/Characteristics:

**b. What do you know of his life story?**

List as many incidents (in the life of David) as you can:

[Invite groups call out their answers and share thoughts.]

Conclude your reflection by summarising the life of David as you see it and why the early Christians were keen to link the genealogy of Jesus to King David.

*David's Family (the tribe of Judah)*

- Father: Jesse (mother not mentioned)

- It is unclear whether David was the seventh son or had seven brothers (1 Samuel 16:10; 1 Chronicles 2:15)

- Two sisters are named Zeruiah and Abigail (1 Chronicles 2:16)

- Wives: Michal (1st wife and younger daughter of King Saul, no children recorded)
The other named wives had children and include: Ahinoam, Abigail, Bathsheba, Maacah, Haggith, Abital, Eglah

- Significant offspring: Amnon, Absalom, Adonijah, Solomon, and Tamar (only daughter with a story).

# 5 — Making Services Meaningful

There is absolutely no point in making services *memorable* unless the service is *meaningful* for that congregation. Making services meaningful involves the heart as well as the head. Worship is not about engaging the body, worship is about engaging the soul.

Engaging heart and soul is a mystical matter that cannot be adequately addressed by a set of suggestions. The word 'God' evokes a wide variety of concepts. Spirituality and spiritual encounters are not the same experience for one person as for another and are not easy to describe or explain. John Wesley famously described such an encounter as feeling his heart strangely warmed. His brother Charles responded to similar profound spiritual experience by writing a hymn.

It is interesting to note that what is known as 'the Wesley Brothers conversion experiences' happened independently and not many days apart. At the Aldersgate meeting John attended, other people heard the same words that John heard, but did not experience what John experienced.

As people we are all different and as lay preachers we will all lead worship differently, not only from ordained preachers, but from other lay preachers. No one preacher will ever connect with all the people all the time. Congregations who have the same preacher in the pulpit every week are not as well served as those who also welcome other preachers. Lay worship leaders may feel they are fill-ins and not as good as the professionals. This may well be true, but it doesn't mean a lay worship leader can't bring something special to a congregation that the congregation values.

As you develop confidence in worship leading you may become comfortable with how you do things and need reminding that confidence breeds complacency. If you are frequently leading services for the same congregation you have a responsibility to those people to not just do what comes naturally to you, but to consider what else these people may need from you.

Self-examination is an element of all spirituality. Understanding where you come from and where you are going is fundamental to leading worship. I know I need reminders. My professional background is in education. My career was teaching kids' stuff and finding creative ways to try and make it stick. If I don't acknowledge my programming I am likely to be snared by it. I enjoy academic stimulation, considering theories, pondering words, developing rituals and directing action. I know I am more comfortable engaging in head stuff and active involvement, than I am at enabling reflective silences.

But I also know reflective silences and stillness are important aspects of spirituality and for some essential for engaging the heart and soul. Without engaging heart and soul, it isn't worship. The prime role of a worship leader is to enable worship.

A service I attended on Low Sunday was led by a retired minster who is a spiritual director. It was a beautiful service, reflective and meaningful. Her message was Christ is alive; open yourself to the risen Christ. One of the ways she exampled this was holding her arms in a gesture of openness when praying. Another was to have us meditate on two very different pictures of resurrection. The first being a stunning explosion of light and colour bursting from the shape of a cross, the other a black and white painting of Christ standing with bowed head in the middle of a dole queue.

One evening I attended an Ephesus group (people who explore all manner of faith concepts). We were treated to an informative reflection on Michael Leunig, and a PowerPoint display of his cartoons discussing what they said to us, rounded off with each of us reading (from a photocopied page) one of his intriguing short prayers. The Low Sunday morning service was in a formal context and focussed on feelings and silences; the evening gathering was informal, directed towards thinking and talking.

Though both were very different I experienced each as meaningful, spiritual events. I also noticed that a lot of careful preparation had been done by both leaders. In attempting to analyse what made these presentations meaningful I have come up with some pointers.

## Pointers for leading spiritual reflections

- Create an atmosphere of togetherness.

- Know your subject.

- Prepare with care.

- Stay focussed on the subject.

- Address the subject from different angles.

- Visuals aid reflection.

- Reflecting requires silence.

## Tips for achieving meaningfulness in services

- Prepare with prayer and diligent research.

- A candle lighting ritual enhances atmosphere.

- Poetry reaches heart and mind.

- Use graphics. Quality pictures can be projected on screen or printed on service sheets.

- Use other helpful visuals: special candles, water in a glass bowl containing pebbles, or floating petals, floating tealight candles, attractive tablecloth, draped fabric.

- Music creates atmosphere. Listen to the musician or recorded music, without singing.

- Singing together unites a group. Ensure the hymns express what you want to convey. If the words can't be sung they can be read in unison.

- Hand holding is a safe and uniting form of physical contact.

- Prepare the people for prayer before praying – have them centre themselves physically and mentally.

  - Physically: Encourage sitting with feet flat on floor and hands positioned to aid praying. For some it may be palms up in openness, for others it may be hands clasped to align the body and express wholeness in holiness.

- Mentally: Invite the people to consider their feelings of this moment and to open themselves to prayer by getting themselves right for prayer.

  Begin praying with words that invite personal prayer beginning with confession, e.g.

  God you know I wish I hadn't done that... or said that..., and that I neglected to do this..., you know I'm sorry. I know you forgive me... Are you nudging me to tell someone else I'm sorry? ...

  Now pray for yourselves ... (time of silence), pray for those closest to you... (time of silence)

  Pray for other you know who need your prayers... (time of silence), Pray for our town... (time of silence), pray for our country... (time of silence), pray for our world... (time of silence)

  We gather our scattered prayers as one by singing the Lord's prayer.

- Pass the Peace after the Lord's Prayer. Rather than greeting lots of people, exchange a few extra words with the those you are engaging with.
- During your reflection – make spaces for silent reflection.

### Meaningful discussions

Discussion groups need to be chaired by a person who makes everyone feel welcome.

It should be made clear that:

- There are no right answers or correct points of view.
- Whatever anyone says will be treated with respect.
- Serious thinking can be aided by humour.
- Reaching consensus and agreed outcomes is not what spirituality is about.
- Questions are more important than answers.

- Opinions are meant to change, explore, enlarge and grow, at a speed and in a direction that fits the individual

These things do not need continual spelling out. Once established they become the group's ethos.

Speakers need to know this is how you operate and that your expectations of the speaker are:

- Information will be imparted in ways that hold the group's attention and invites interaction.

- Participation activities are encouraged and so is reflective silence.

Speakers, even if known by the group, need introducing with due respect.

What is needed should be ready – whiteboard, projector, table, chair, lectern, water etc.

The chairperson is responsible for ensuring the meeting finishes on time and the speaker thanked

Eating together afterwards enhances fellowship.

End with a short reflective or commission type prayer such as this:

> May the Christ who walks on wounded feet
> walk with us on the road;
> May the Christ who loves with wounded hands
> stretch out our hands to serve;
> May the Christ who loves with wounded heart,
> open our hearts to love;
> May we see the face of Christ in everyone we meet;
> And may everyone we meet see the face of Christ in us.
>
> *Traditional Celtic prayer*

# 6 — How to organise a church service

## 1. Check exactly what is required of you

- Are you responsible for the entire service or will other people be involved?
- Is there anything that should be acknowledged on this particular Sunday?
- When does the church's office require your 'Order of Service'?
- Who contacts the organist and Bible readers?

If the church or venue is unfamiliar to you, confirm these details:

- Time and place of service, parking provision, and what is required of you?
- Is a printed service bulletin or a PowerPoint used?
- Is there anything that should be mentioned for this church on this particular Sunday?
- Are there any set opening or closing rituals such as candle-lighting, bringing the Bible in and out; acknowledging birthdays; passing the peace, singing a three-fold amen or a particular blessing etc.?
- Is there a minister's steward or someone expecting to pray with you before the service?

It is usual for a local person to introduce a visiting worship leader and give the notices. Some congregations have lay people regularly doing other worship tasks such as taking children's slot, giving the 'Pastoral Prayers' or presenting a musical item.

Inquire as to:

- Usual size of the congregation?
- Likelihood of children being present?
- What hymn book is used?
- How the music is provided?
- How the musician and readers are contacted?

## 2. Check the Lectionary

The Lectionary informs which season of the church year is being celebrated and what readings are recommended for each Sunday of the year. The Lectionary also notes special Sundays that may be celebrated throughout the year and may offer additional readings to suit that particular celebration, e.g. Home and Family Sunday.

## 3. Read all the set readings

Think on them in a prayerful attitude. Four readings are offered for each Sunday. All may be used in the service but only two are required, normally one from the 'Old Testament' (often now called the 'Hebrew Scriptures') and one from the New Testament.

You do not have to use the set readings, but don't ignore the lectionary without a very good reason.

## 4. Select Bible passages

When you have chosen a passage that 'speaks to you' research the passage thoroughly to enable you to 'speak it to others.' Read your selection in different Bible translations, consult relevant devotional books and Bible commentaries or do some research online. It is important to decide on your theme early in the week to match your theme with a children's slot ('Family Time') and find suitable hymns and prayers.

### Bible-Gateway – versions of the Bible online

This free website www.biblegateway.com is user-friendly and great for finding Bible passages. If you want your readers to use a particular Bible translation, copy the passage from the website and email it to the readers.

### Printing out Bible passages offers advantages:

The script can be produced in any size print. Ordinary Bibles often have very small print.

Verses can be deleted where omitted in the lectionary. This removes a potential difficulty.

Extra relevant verses can easily be added.

If a passage lends itself to a dramatised reading by two or more readers, words in speech marks can be highlighted for the different readers.

## 5. Find suitable hymns and prayers

Hymns and prayers should fit the theme of your service and complement your 'sermon' (now commonly called a 'reflection'). The 'order of service' is usually produced as a paper bulletin or as a PowerPoint. The church office is likely to require this in its final form by Wednesday. You do not need to have your sermon/reflection completed before the service sheet is finalised, as long as you know your topic and where you are going with it.

## 6. Things to check near end of week

- That the person providing the music is happy with your choices?
- That the office has produced what you wanted?
- That the readers have their readings?

## Services in General

There are various types of church services that range from very formal to very informal, serving different purposes to meet varying needs of particular congregations. Each type of service has its own pattern of being. This book will look at different approaches but will begin with the service lay people are most often called to lead – filling in for an absent minister or presbyter on an ordinary Sunday. This normally requires leading a typical formal service.

## Formal Services

A formal service can be considered a piece of drama that follows a set choreography. Each part of the service is designed to contribute to the whole production that aims to be a thing of beauty, that gathers those present into a heightened state of spiritual awareness. The words spoken and music selected should be done with care.

There is space for informality during the time of greeting and in the children's or family time segment. However, most of the service should follow written words, particularly when being led by an inexperienced worship leader. This applies to the liturgy and the reflection.

### A Worship Leader's preparation prayer

> Keep me mindful O God that it is you who has called me to lead and interpret your Holy Scripture. I seek the inspiration and discernment that will enable me to do this task to the best of my ability.
>
> Help me share the holy stories in ways that speak to the people of today. Guide me to choose what is helpful for this particular congregation, the people of _____. Help me to see the wider picture and to present the details of liturgy and sermon with connection and creativity.
>
> Grant me sufficient confidence and humility to do the task well, and the grace to uphold your sacred trust. Amen.

## Order of Service

The 'programme' of a service varies from church to church but differences are usually minor and relate mostly to the initial welcome, position of the notices, whether there is a music item, and how children are catered for. Some churches have their own small rituals such as bringing the Bible in and out, candle lighting, acknowledging birthdays, sharing significant events, passing the peace with a handshake, singing a particular blessing or holding hands for The Grace.

### A typical formal service follows this pattern

The printed service sheet usually has its own Parish heading. Beneath this is printed the date and Sunday of the Lectionary Calendar (e.g. 'Advent 3') and the names of the worship leader and organist.

| | |
|---|---|
| **Greetings and notices** | Welcome everyone. Invite visitors to introduce themselves. |
| **Call to worship** | Introductory statement. Some words may be read by congregation |
| **1st Hymn** | Begin with a well-known hymn that sets the scene for the theme. |
| **Prayer of Approach** | Prayer relating to theme, with some congregational responses. |
| **Family Time** | Informal message delivered via story, chat, illustrations or activity. |
| **2nd Hymn** | Children's hymn or a lively new hymn relating to the 'family time' message. |
| **Creative Presentation** | Group or solo music; poem; dance; meditation; famous prayer etc. |
| **Readings** | The Old Testament reading should be given before the New Testament reading. |
| **3rd Hymn** | Meditative hymn that introduces the Reflection. |
| **Reflection** | Bible based message usually delivered in the manner of a formal speech. |
| **Offering** | Dedication prayer, which may either be read by worship leader or by everyone. |
| **Pastoral Prayers** | Longest prayer time, with space for silent prayer and the Lord's Prayer. |
| **4th Hymn** | Relates to the reflection. A well-known tune makes for a good ending. |
| **Benediction/ Commission** | Said with congregation standing and eyes open. |
| **Sung Amen or Sung Blessing** | Or set spoken words. Some congregations like to link hands. |

# 7 — Lectionary and Liturgy

**The Lectionary** is the worship leader's primary resource. All worship leaders should be provided with a copy by their parish. Failing this it can be found on the national Church's website.

Become very familiar with the opening pages that explain the Calendar (liturgical seasons) and the composition of the lectionary. The Common Lectionary is used by most traditional Christian denominations all over the world. Most churches throughout Christendom are likely to be using the same text on any given Sunday.

The Lectionary and Liturgical Year follow a pattern. The Great Festivals of the Christian Year are Christmas, Easter and Pentecost. Each Festival has its own special season of Advent, Christmas, Epiphany, Lent, Easter and Pentecost, followed by Ordinary Time.

Lesser rituals include: Harvest Festival, Mother's Day (now 'Home and Family Sunday'), Disability Sunday etc. and also local festivals such as Saints Days, Spring Flower Sunday, Animal Blessings etc. All the main special services are detailed in the Lectionary. All rituals that acknowledge seasons or subjects in a spiritual way give added shape and meaning to worship.

**Lectionary readings** follow a prescribed pattern. The Revised Common Lectionary (1992) follows a three-year cycle with a particular Gospel given prominence each year. Year A is Matthew, Year B Mark and Year C Luke. These three are called the Synoptic Gospels as they share some of the same texts and appear to have drawn on a common source. The Gospel of John is quite different in format and its reflective content gets worked into the other years particularly during the seasons of Lent and Easter.

Regardless of it being Year A, B or C, Epiphany comes in January and is followed by the Baptism of Jesus followed by the Temptations, the Call of the Disciples, and then the Ministry of Jesus. It is a natural progression. The Gospel Readings are contextually linked to the other Lectionary Readings for the day.

**The Liturgy** refers to the set prayers and the order they come in the service.

It is usual for the liturgy to include words spoken by the congregation as well as the leader.

Some traditional prayers have set responses or refrains for the congregation, but any prayer can be turned into a responsive prayer by printing suitable lines or phrases in bold print.

Antiphonal prayers are similar except the alternative lines come from the two sides of the church.

Involving the congregation helps keep people focussed (and saves the preacher's voice).

Sitting, standing and kneeling, while adding meaning also have the practical purpose of enabling people to move physically and thus be more attentive.

Choose your prayers with care.

Unless they are traditional prayers from a past era, ensure the wording reflects a theology suitable for today's understandings.

### Be Gender Inclusive

- People in general should not be referred to as man, men, brother, brethren or mankind.

- Use all people, persons, friends, folk, brothers and sisters, family of God, humankind or humanity.

- Do not call a group of children 'guys' (though seen as friendly, it is sexist). Use children, boys and girls, little people (for small children), young people or young folks (for mixed ages).

- Jesus or Christ is always referred to in masculine terms.

- The Holy Spirit can be female or male.

- God is beyond gender, but via Jewish patriarchy is traditionally considered male.

- If your preference is gender neutral use terms, such as: Loving God, Dear God, Creator God, Mother and Father of us all, Our Parent God; substitute male pronouns with the words God and Godself.

See also Chapter 19 — Sample Prayers.

# 8 — How to prepare a reflection (sermon)

Many regular church goers feel quite able to lead a worship service, except for 'the sermon bit.' This is the section that stops potential worship leaders volunteering for the task. It is the one piece of the service that can't be taken from a book. A reflection requires something personal from the person who presents it. For the committed Christian it is a very meaningful exercise that helps you explore and firm up on what you believe. In writing and preaching it you may be able to help others.

Preparing a reflection is not difficult but it does take time and effort.

In the 'good old days' there was a simple formula for parsons preparing sermons: State your text (usually a single verse) and from it deliver three points. Parsons needed a clear and simple guide, as most led three services a Sunday with two of them being to the same congregation.

Today's worship leaders are not given a formula to follow. The expectation is that a passage, or related passages, of scripture will be explored and the findings presented as a useful message.

As lay preachers we usually have at least a month to mull over our reflection. It is a big advantage we have over clergy, who need to produce at least one sermon a week.

Preparing a reflection should be done in a prayerful way as we are seeking to present God's truth to an audience. But your thinking, researching and writing is more likely to happen spasmodically than in one sitting, so it may be helpful to have 'arrow prayers' ready to fire at random thoughts, such as:

> God, direct my research and understanding.

> God, help me use this in the light of your wisdom.

> Help me craft my words with care, so those who listen
> will your truth hear.

A reflection is not intended to be based on a single verse. A reflection looks at a passage of scripture and sets it in context, drawing on other texts, related quotations, stories, and experiences to deliver a message of relevance for the hearers.

***Ask yourself: What is the message I am trying to present?***
Begin by asking these key basic questions of the Bible passage:

- When was this written?

- Why was it written?

- Who was it written for?

- What may it be saying to us in our context?

To find good answers you must do some research. If serious about worship leading you will invest in some good printed resources. However, there is a plethora of Bible resources freely available online. With the lectionary recycling every three years, there are many lectionary-based sermons posted on the web. Choose your sources with care. Just as a lot of nonsense is spouted by the religious channels on TV, a lot of nonsense is pushed by dodgy theologians in cyberspace.

Ask your presbyter or a knowledgeable mentor to direct you to good sources that have the respect of your denomination. (See the list at the end of this book)

Although you need to have answers to the basic key questions, you do not have to express them as a formula. Your task is to present a meaningful message. The questions serve to focus you on the Bible text. How you express your understandings is up to you. Like a good novel, a good sermon should begin with an opening sentence that arouses interest in what is to follow.

It is important to give context to the passage being explored but keep mindful that modern audiences learn through entertainment and engagement. 'Reflection entertainment' comes in various forms: a statement that produces a wry smile; a joke that brings a chuckle; a meditation that arouses a sense of connection; stories that evoke passion, or heightened awareness. Information, when interesting and relevant, also counts as entertainment. Education is a continuing process in all areas of life. In our time of incredible knowledge expansion that 'old time religion' is not good enough for us. The information explosion of today challenges everything. We live in exciting times. New concepts about God and religion are exciting and essential. To make a better world we have to find the best ways of using all new information.

If your reflection fails to entertain and engage, your message is unlikely to be grasped. However, few parishioners would say the reason they attend church is to be entertained. People have various reasons for attending church but for most there is a hope of being nourished spiritually and to feel closer to God by being part of a faith community. Never lose sight of the fact that the Christian faith community is based on the teachings of Jesus.

In my youth I used to enjoy visiting different churches with some of my peers. I have forgotten where in New Zealand this church was but something I perceived as inspirational lodged in my memory. The pulpit was up a few steps and on the small landing wall where the steps turned to the pulpit were the words in gold letters, "Sir, show us Jesus." I recognised the words as relating to an incident (recorded in John's Gospel: 12:21) when some Greeks visiting Jerusalem for Passover heard of Jesus. They went to Philip asked him where they could see Jesus. I remember thinking what inspirational words these were for a preacher to read every time he (all the preachers I knew at the time were male) was about to speak to a congregation.

The purpose of the ordinary Sunday sermon is to 'preach the Gospel' and this can only be achieved by showing Jesus. In practical terms it means discussing Scripture in a manner that promotes understanding of the teachings of Jesus. Showing Jesus doesn't mean that the Hebrew Scriptures (Old Testament) should be ignored. Jesus grew up with these scriptures and they formed the foundation of his teaching. These ancient Hebrew stories have become so entwined with western culture that they are an important part of our cultural heritage, referred to in literature and in common speech. The old stories also carry our formative concepts of God and spirituality.

It is important to be sensitive to your congregation. A congregation is comprised of individuals who bring with them a wide range of experiences and theological understanding. Few are likely to have exactly the same ideas of God and theology as you hold. Everyone's reality is different. And everyone is on a different stage of their spiritual journey. Good people can believe very different things about the reality of God. Accept that what a person believes can be right for them, even if it isn't right for you.

Some members of your congregation will be content with a predominantly literal concept of the Bible they feel has served them well, but more will be searching for ways to make their beliefs relevant to life as they experience it in the 21st century. Pushing boundaries is never well served by pushing people into corners. In matters concerning spirituality and faith there is always room for mystery.

The lay preacher's role is not to condemn or offend. Nor should you 'talk down' to your listeners. You are not a teacher instructing a class of infants. Your adult congregation are experienced thinkers. The lay preacher's job is to explore scripture and offer faith thoughts relevant to the hearers. For myself I try do this in ways that nurture, stimulate, and challenge.

Don't set yourself up as an authority. Even experts do not agree on Biblical scholarship or issues relating to God and faith. When offering a reflection use phrases like: some scholars say...; there are various theories and this is an interesting one...; I find it helpful to...

You can't speak for the reality of others you can only speak of your own reality. You don't have to bare all, but be honest in what you do say. Being honest does not require making statements that belittle what others believe. Be up front with what is important to you but make it Ok for others to have different opinions. If you don't expect all your listeners to agree with you, you may be pleasantly surprised how many say things like: that really gave me something to think about, I found what you said very interesting ... could I have a copy of your sermon.

## Content of a Reflection in brief

- Begin with an interesting opening.

- Set the context of the passage.

- Develop your theme through story, anecdote and quotations.

- Draw from the historic significance, significance for our times.

- Say what you feel the Bible message means for you.

- Offer a challenge for the congregation to consider.

## Practical considerations

A sermon / reflection is normally between 1,000 and 2,000 words. Don't be content with your first effort, mull over it for several days and keep refining what you have written. Reading your reflection aloud will help you to spot grammatical errors and weak points.

Check that your language is gender inclusive; the words flow well; borrowed words are acknowledged; you have included pertinent anecdotes or something personal; there is a logical thought progression that leads to a sound conclusion that relates to the teachings of Jesus.

Print your script in a font and size that is easy for you to read, e.g. 14 or 16 point. Use spaced paragraphing. Read your reflection out loud and time yourself. A traditional service is an hour long, people feel cheated if it takes much less and annoyed if it takes much longer. Getting the timing right is a skill that takes practise.

### *Presentation*

Some preachers prefer not to stand in the pulpit, but be aware it is important that everyone can see you and hear you. There is nothing more frustrating for elderly church goers than being isolated through not seeing or hearing. Always use a microphone if it is available and speak slower than in conversational speech. Give your words time to sink in. Make eye contact in the pauses. If there is no microphone, remember to throw your voice to the back of the church and keep the volume up at the end of sentences.

While varying the volume you speak at to dramatise your text, keep your energy level up and stay focussed throughout the sermon. It is easy for your voice to  drop unintentionally.

Make sure some A5 service sheets are printed as A4 for people with vision problems.

> Note: A sermon / reflection does not have to be one person speaking for 20 minutes. The bulk of a reflection can be presented as a dialogue, or a play reading, or by persons reading short poems and meditations that the worship leader ties together with a few well-chosen words. Involvement of others is enriching and memorable. The down-side is it takes even more time and effort to prepare than writing a full-length reflection.

# 9 — Service sheets and PowerPoints

Most churches which do not have their own prayer book use either a printed service sheet or a PowerPoint to help the congregation to follow what is happening within the service, and enable active participation in the liturgy. It is therefore vital that all can see the words.

### Printed sheets

The font needs to be clear and large with responses in bold print. If a folded bulletin of A5 size pages is used it is important to cater for vision impaired people by enlarging some pages to A4 size. These usually work better as single sheets stapled.

Be mindful that each piece of paper costs the church and, as there has to be enough for everyone, there will be some left over. Churches have their own protocols regards the number of sheets used. One sheet of A4 printed landscape and folded in half gives four A5 pages. This will not allow you to print all your hymns and prayers in full. Even 2 sheets of A4 and the resulting 8 A5 pages may not be enough to provide large enough print. So, you have to be selective. Enhance the text with illustrations where space permits.

### What not to print

If you have a responsive Call to Worship, you may not need a responsive prayer of Approach. The Pastoral Prayers are usually not printed, but as is traditional in a prayer of petition a refrain can be printed with the lead in phrase and response, e.g. "Lord hear our prayer ... **And grant us your mercy.**" The offertory prayer does not have to be printed but, as it is a short prayer and the congregation have stood for it, it is good to include this if space allows. The traditional Lord's Prayer does not need to be printed. However, modern paraphrases of the prayer should be printed or projected. Hymns from your church hymnal do not need to be printed.

### Inclusive language in Hymns

Some preachers want to make the language of hymns gender inclusive or neutral and to print out hymns from the hymnal in order to adjust the words. Do this with caution. Rhyme, rhythm and atmosphere must be considered. To make the word 'man' inclusive is a major problem. Man is a one syllable word than rhymes with many words. The only one syllable inclusive substitute is 'folk', which rhymes with very little and does not carry the same dignity as 'man' did in previous times.

The word 'God' is less of a problem as by itself it is gender inclusive. Also, God rhymes with very few appropriate words and therefore is not often at the end of a line. The difficulty comes with the attached male pronouns – he, him, and himself. Those who prefer not to use these in relation to God can simply sing 'God' or 'Godself' when these pronouns appear.

Of greater concern is the vexing issue that hymns from the past often promote a theology that is not suitable for today, and that the imagery relates the northern hemisphere, particularly for Christmas or Easter. However, many of our people connect to them through nostalgia and a love of the old tunes. Hymns from the past have a place in contemporary services – a shrinking place. Use them sparingly and drop the verses that have no merit.

I work on the premise that if the hymn was written before the mid-20th century the author presumed his/her words were inclusive. Later lyric writers should know better, and I won't use their hymns if they are not gender inclusive. The great thing is we have hundreds of wonderful New Zealand hymns available to us that are gender inclusive and that draw on Southern Hemisphere imagery. So always include some local hymns. The more you use them, the better loved they will become.

## PowerPoints

PowerPoints have the presentation advantages of little cost and unlimited space for both text and pictures. Do not get carried away with the creative potential. The text has to be clear and uncluttered. Do not print hymns or prayers on top of photos. Make sure you, as worship leader, do not block the screen and that people who have to remain seated can see the screen. The downside of going paper-less is the congregation has nothing to take home with them for further reflection, or to remind of notices and church contacts. These things should be provided for in some other way.

Remember to get your order of service to the church office early in the week to give the staff sufficient time to produce a copy you can check before the final printing.

## No service sheet or PowerPoint

There are some small congregations that do not have access to a church office with a photocopier or PowerPoint expertise. This is not a big worry. Preachers have only had these aids for a very short time in the history of church services. Print out your own order of service for yourself to follow. Many churches have their own printed resource folder that contains a selection of prayers and new hymns. Standard church hymnals usually include some printed prayers or psalms. Verses of some hymns can be read as prayers. This can be done antiphonally with the two sides of the church reading alternative lines, or alternating male and female voices. If there is anything you particularly want the congregation to say or sing you can easily print off copies yourself and hand them out. Congregations without offices are small in size, so you won't need many copies.

## Time considerations and setting up

Allow yourself plenty of time so you do not arrive in a state of rush and panic.

(But, don't arrive ridiculously early – waiting around with nothing to do, or having to make lengthy small talk, can also be panic inducing).

You may be met by 'the minister's steward' who will give any help you need and will pray with you in private room before the service. Most churches ensure someone is on duty to care for you, though it may be a person who is also on door duty.

Set up your worship materials in the pulpit or lectern if this where the service is led from. If given a choice I go for the pulpit as there is more space for concealing gear.

- Check that you have been provided with a fresh glass of water and a hymn book.

- Check in with 'the team' who are helping to create this service of worship, including:

- People on the door who hand out the hymn books and service sheets

- The sound system person (you may need to be fitted with a lapel microphone)

- Others who may want to confirm such things as notices; candle lighting; where to place the Bible etc.

- Exchange words of greeting with the organist and check all is OK music wise.

Start on time. Some churches get lax with their starting time. Make it clear when you are leading the service you expect it to start on time. You only have an hour to fit everything in. Your commitment is to end on time.

Some congregations expect to shake hands with the worship leader on the way out, others don't. If shaking hands, make sure you aren't blocking those who are trying to get to the after-service cuppa. Standing by the door is usually best. Try to thank all who have helped with the service.

# 10 — The Preacher's Satchel

It is useful to keep a separate bag, satchel or briefcase for worship.

## Permanent contents should include:

### Personal items

| | |
|---|---|
| Small pack of tissues | You never know when a tissue may be needed. |
| Throat lozenges | A tickle in your throat is distressing for everyone. |
| Comb | Hair can get very messed up getting from car to church on a windy, wet day. |

### Pen and paper

You may be given last minute notices, prayer requests, and names of visitors to welcome. It is also useful to jot down the names of the children present, if the opportunity presents.

### Items that cater for unexpected children

You must have a children's picture book that contains a good message. Choose one with bright illustrations and not many words. If you didn't plan for a children's slot, you need to be conscious of the extra time you are taking.

It is useful to have a small object that you know how to use to illustrate an impromptu children's talk.

Include a few activity sheets and small supply of pencils and felt-pens or crayons

### A full set of prayers that will suit any service

It is always possible that the service sheets fail to arrive, or there is a malfunction of the PowerPoint. Even with no technical hitches it is also possible that some part of the liturgy was missed off the service sheet or PowerPoint. Even if you checked them, you may have failed to notice the omission until the service is underway.

I carry two full sets of prayers stapled to A4 sized sheets of cardboard. This gives me a choice of appropriate prayers and keeps the pages in good condition while making them easy to find in an emergency. It is important to include the Lord's Prayer. You may think you know it inside out, but when leading a congregation memory can falter or you may slide into another version that confuses everyone.

## If travelling beyond your home parish

Check the route and how long it should take you to get there.

Allow plenty of time. You can always wait nearby if you arrive too early.

Make sure you have the details of who to call should you be unexpectedly delayed by traffic or some other possible, albeit unlikely, emergency.

# 11 — Children's Time / Family Time

Catering for children is tricky. The age range can be vast. Some congregations do not have children attending on a regular basis. Others have some on their pastoral roll, but attendance is spasmodic. Some always have children present.

## Children always present

The worship leader comes prepared with a story or activity that relates to the theme of the service.

## No children expected

Where churches have no registered children the traditional children's slot can be replaced with an adult creative slot. This can be an informal time of adult sharing or adult education; or a formal time of appreciating a musical item, a poem, mediation or famous prayer. However, the worship leader needs to be prepared for the appearance of an unexpected child or children (see 'the preacher's satchel').

## Often present but not always

My way of coping with this is to replace 'The Children's Talk' with 'Family Time.'

## Family Time

The intention of the slot is to direct attention towards the theme of the adult service in ways that can include children. Adults and children are encouraged to participate in the conversation but a better way to engage with children is through action. Just like adults, children do not enjoy questions that put them 'on the spot.' Invite the children to help you by: holding things, showing things, moving things, miming actions or playing a game.

Family Time should be informal and creative. The worship leader speaks without notes and seeks active, spontaneous interaction with the congregation. Problems can be posed, information given, stories told, and visual aids used to good effect, but the message should also fit the adult focus. Don't get over complicated when presenting this segment. You are aiming to get across one basic message. If you feel you can't present the children's / family time without notes, re-work the concept until you can.

To simply read a story to the children reduces Family Time to Children's Time, which is OK, as adults will accept not seeing or hearing for a short period. When reading a picture book, the children need to be clustered around you. This involves direct interaction that can help you develop confidence for talking without a script. Stories that are read require a spoken introduction.

Make your introduction interactive by asking a couple of questions, e.g. Can anyone read the name of this book? Do you think this is an old story or a modern story? Why do you think that? What do you think this story is going to be about? A spoken conclusion isn't necessary as a good story speaks for itself but if you want to have more interaction, ask: what was your favourite part of this story or what could we learn from this story? Hints may be needed. Praise answers. If none are forthcoming from the children, ask the adults.

If your church provides materials for children to draw pictures, ask for ideas or suggest what to draw. As an alternative provide your own photocopied worksheets that complement the story. Be sure to invite the children forward just before the end of the service to show everyone what they have done.

See also Chapter 16 — Sample 'Family Time' slots and Chapter 18 — Ideas for Devotions, Family Time and less formal services.

# 12 — Circle and Cafe style services

For a long time, there has been a move away from fixed pews set in rigid rows. Flexibility was the cry. Many churches ditched their pews and replaced them with more comfortable chairs, set out in the same rows. The more daring opted for a multi-layered semicircle that gave a feeling of greater intimacy, that not all were comfortable with, and the service continued as it always had.

Some folk who enjoyed facing each other in worship began experimenting with alternative services held in the church hall or lounge with the chairs set out in a single circle or around tables. The intention was to combine fellowship with worship. This called for a less formal service and greater congregational participation. These services were usually held at a different time to the main service.

Falling roll numbers and earthquake damaged churches has meant a radical rethink of worship, hence the increasing popularity of circle or cafe style services.

## Leading an Alternative Service

Alternative services develop their own ways of being and like any other service you need to know what is required of you. Even if the service follows the usual hymn / prayer sandwich, you will have greater flexibility in presenting your message.

Tables enable a wide range of creative small group activities. But a circle of chairs can easily be moved into groups of 2–4 and quickly moved back into the circle. If writing is required, provide each group with a clipboard, pen and paper or just a book to write on.

# Activities

- Leader led discussion with the whole group. A white-board is useful but not essential.

- Discussion in pairs or small groups, sharing opinions or experiences.

- Answer a set of questions. The 'when, who, why, what' questions fit all Bible texts.

- Compare Bible passages

- Reflect on pictures. What message was intended by artist or photographer? What is your reaction?

- Creating posters or murals.

- Placemat activities. Print a set of focussed activities and pictures for each person, e.g.

  - Individual Bible word-searches.

  - Group Bible puzzle.

  - Tabletop models, e.g. create a bridge from ice-cream sticks and plasticine – an exercise in planning and cooperation.

  - Create a ship or train from packets, cardboard rolls etc. held together with sellotape. Explain how this could be a symbol for the church.

  - Construct a well or wall from brown cardboard cartons and / or shoeboxes. With vivid markers add words that explain or summarise the message.

- Use the flexible space for activities that involve movement:

  - Action songs

  - Creative Dance

  - Mime

  - Unrehearsed play readings – see the author's book, Ten Plays: *Short, easy dramas for churches.*

## Materials

### Essential
A supply of white A4 paper, pens, pencils, felt-pens or crayons and vivid markers .

### Useful
Small scissors, glue, staplers, white-board and markers, and clipboards if there are no tables

Magazines to cut up: *Listener, National Geographic,* women's magazines.

Pictures for reflection: *Touchstone, Spanz, Tui Motu* magazine, Bible pictures, Christmas cards, calendars, supply of coloured paper. Also a few cardboard templates for children to trace round to add extra interest to their pictures.

Cardboard templates: Copy simple line drawings from a Bible sticker book onto card, cut out the shapes, add a few details with felt pen.

Uses: For Palm Sunday provide donkey and foal templates and sheets of grey paper. Children draw a Palestine street scene (or landscape) on white paper, then trace round donkey shapes on grey paper, cut them out, and glue them to the drawing.

There are various Bible stories where donkey shapes can be used in this way. Black camel shapes look good silhouetted against a sunset. Angel shapes on yellow paper go well on a black sky.

For examples of Cafe Services see Chapter 17 — Sample Cafe Services.

# 13 — Services for rest homes

Lay worship leaders may be called upon to lead services in rest homes. The type of service required differs from home to home depending on the local tradition of that place and the residents who attend.

Some may be predominantly incapacitated cognitively; other congregations may have people who appreciate intellectual stimulation. The time slot allocated also varies but is more likely to be 30 minutes than 60. You need to know how the music is provided and what hymn book is used. It is important to get a feel for the place before leading a service.

The best way to achieve this is to begin by being a support person for others experienced in leading services at this home. It is helpful to all involved if you have got to know some of the residents in the capacity of a pastoral visitor.

Broadly speaking there are two types of rest home services, formal and less formal.

## Formal services

Formal services offer comfort in the known. This is particularly important for residents who have short term memory loss. The old well-known hymns, prayers and readings usually serve these people best. These people grew up in an era when the King James Version of the Bible and its Lord's Prayer were read and said at school assemblies.

For these people your message will be the least important part of the service and they won't remember it. What you say needs to be short. That said they deserve a message that holds their attention for the moment in a way that is meaningful. Where possible, go visual. If there is no set place of worship, set up a worship table. Use fabric, candles, flowers etc for a focus. Set up an appropriate display for the season or message. Illustrate your message with a large picture, poster or article where possible.

## Less formal services

Less formal services should offer the traditional comforts as above but allow for a more innovative approach. Illustrate you message with objects that you can hold up or pass around the group.

It may be possible to involve the residents in discussions, such as: sharing experiences of their Sunday School and Bible Class days, what faith has meant to them in their lives, their favourite hymns and why a particular hymn is meaningful to them and teach a new hymn (Colin Gibson's *How much am I worth* is ideal for elderly folk).

All services can be enhanced by providing a musical item, e.g. solo, small choir, guitar or a recording. The mere presence of well-behaved children is uplifting but some youngsters have talents that can be used within the service (reading a meditation, singing, playing an instrument, creative dance etc.). I recommend that you find ways of involving the children of your church, including groups that meet in your church hall.

It can be helpful to think of the 'reflection' part of rest home services as 'devotions' and not as a 'sermon.' Examples of devotions and family time talks are provided in Chapters 14 and 18.

## Tips for connecting with seniors

- Speak very clearly.
- Introduce yourself.
- Make eye contact and smile.
- Welcome everyone warmly.
- Make concluding pleasantries to the group, e.g. It is lovely to see you all, I'm so glad you were able to be here today, Next week the service will be led by _____, I am looking forward to being with you when it is my turn again. Try to greet each person individually.
- Physical contact in the form of a handshake or touch on the arm is usually appreciated.
- 'Talking down' is not appreciated.
- Use Mr, Mrs, Miss or Ms titles unless you are invited to use first names.
- Do not patronise anyone by calling them 'dear' or 'love.'

# 14 — Devotions: Ideas to build on

Devotions usually comprise a brief mediation, prayer, and sometimes a hymn, at the beginning of a meeting. Though short in duration all devotions begin from a theme or an idea, which is also how all sermons begin. Inspiration always begins with an idea. Devotions are ripe with potential for developing into rest home and cafe services.

The content of devotions often centres on a single inspirational message. To develop this message into a sermon / reflection you need to connect the theme with a Biblical concept that 'shows Jesus' by relating in some manner, to the Way of Christ. To expand devotions into a service you will need to find more prayers and hymns (or recorded music) to fit your theme. Augment the message with additional poems and mediations. Don't forget congregational participation. Question and answers, comments and sharing, can happily happen as a group or with the person sitting next to you. Cafe services are ideal for active and creative participation. Be innovative. But, first you need a theme.

## Themes to get you thinking

| | |
|---|---|
| Gardens | Planned places created to enjoy, upkeep requires work and water. |
| Wisdom | Consider what wisdom is and where it is found? |
| Journeys | The journey of life; pilgrimages; journeys of Bible characters. |
| Wind | Link with flight, kite, sailing, spreading seeds and the Holy Spirit. |
| Rivers | Life-giving, their place in nature, how valued by us. Name your special river and share why; explore the importance of the Jordan river in Jewish religious understanding. |
| Mountains | Consider their grandeur, name a mountain special to you and share why. Give the Māori mihimihi greeting and introduction. |

| | |
|---|---|
| Trees | Their many varieties and many uses. |
| Flowers | Study a flower intently, wonder at the intricacy of its beauty, describe in detail. |
| Families | Complexities and joys, families of childhood, families formed as adults. |
| Names | Your name, why was it given and what it means. Bible names and their meanings. |
| Candles | Ancient, fragile light made by layering wax on string, symbol of God's presence. |
| Stars | The night sky, star realities, fantasy and symbolism; people who are stars; Matariki. |
| Travellers | Share travel experiences, reflect on inspirations gained. |
| Missions | Missions – international, local and personal. |
| Prayer | Different ways of praying. What prayer means to you? Famous prayers. |
| Faith | What is it, where is it seen, how do we share it? |
| Celebrations | Big and small, why, what and how we celebrate? What is the purpose of the celebration? |
| Proverbs | Quote common proverbs. Discuss the book of Proverbs. |
| Favourite Texts | Recall memories of learning or hearing. Quote John 3:16 and 23rd Psalm together. |
| Inspirational Quotations | Listen to a selection. Chose a quote to print on a stone or make into a poster. |
| Spring | Consider the symbolism of renewed warmth and growth. |
| Summer | The opportunities of summer. Share what summer means to you? |
| Autumn | Associate falling leaves and planting bulbs with death and resurrection. |
| Winter | Relate to the special joys that winter brings – frost, snow and cosy times. |

# 15 — Complete Service Samples

## Complete Service Sample 1 — The Season of Lent

**Call to worship:**

> Kia ora tātou!
> **Kia ora**
>
> Today is the first Sunday in Lent
> **We remember the wilderness experience**
> **that ultimately led Jesus to the cross.**
>
> We remember that Christ struggled
> with thoughts of the future
> But he remained true and
> did not falter in follow his calling
> **We have struggles and temptations in our lives**
> **We come to you for inner strength and**
> **the power of the Spirit**
>
> We come to worship God.

**Hymn:** *Come, thou long expected Jesus* With One Voice 200.
(Words: Charles Wesley)

**Prayer of Approach:**

> In this season of struggle,
> we accept the invitation to re-examine our faith.
> Our desire is for the message of Christmas
> – peace, hope, love and joy,
> but we live in a world of unlimited possibilities,
> and you gave us freedom.
> Part of our freedom lies in the reality
> of sword, money, and dice.
> Lent is not a comfortable time.
> **Help us use Lent well.**

**Give us insight into ourselves
and help us understand the reality of others.**

You know our strengths and our weaknesses.
**But we come knowing ourselves
to be sons and daughters.**

Your love knows us, judges us, and keeps us.
**Keep us true to Christ, so that we may be true to
ourselves and true to others.
Help us do justice to your holiness,
and serve your eternal purpose.**

Gracious God,
you have brought us into the richness of faith:
**Our hope for the future exists
in the continuing tragedy and triumph
of love as we see love
through Jesus Christ our Lord. Amen**

**Family time: Being attentive.** (What is missing from church today?)

**Hymn:** *Mine eyes have seen the glory.* With One Voice 205.
(Words: Julia Ward Howe. Tune (ii): John Brown's Body)

**Readings:**

> Genesis 7:1–5; 9:18–28
> Mark 1:1–13

**Poem:** *Temptation* by Maren Tirabassi

> And Mark, who was first to write,
> says — Jesus was tempted,
> not listing any particular temptations,
> and so, later,
> Matthew and Luke suggested
> power over food, glory,
> and personal safety as good examples.
>
> As a woman, I am more often
> tempted by my need to be loved,
> self-diminishment,
> and protecting someone dear.

79

All six would have damaged the ministry.
I applaud Mark's resisting the … temptation
to fill in the blanks,

because what I need for living
is that Jesus was tempted
and made it,
so whenever
the diva in the mind or
the hound in the heart
sets as a trap,
I can make it, too,

and I will have as my companions,
animals and angels.

## Reflection: The Season of Lent

[Year B lectionary-based reflection that draws on
personal reflection of contemporary issues and
knowledge retained from past Bible Study.]

Lent – a religious season of preparation, self-examination, and facing hard questions.

I intend so to do. But, I will begin with a light-hearted question: Do you ever watch the Father Brown Mysteries?

Kindly priest and amateur sleuth, Father Brown solves the surprising number of murders that occur within his picturesque village parish. In an episode I watched recently he was about to conduct a funeral. As the casket was carried into the church a knocking came from inside the casket. The ensuing alarm brought the funeral to an urgent halt. While some mourners were proclaiming a miracle Father Brown replied, "While I can't completely rule out a supernatural resurrection I would be more inclined to go for a rational explanation first."

The script-writers certainly expected the viewers to side with Father Brown. Had we been given a supernatural explanation I would have felt cheated, wouldn't you?

But I don't deny that humans can relate to mystical experiences. Late December last year a story broke on National News about a controversial walking track up Te Mata Peak in the Craggy Range

Winery. New Zealand is becoming increasingly covered by spectacular walking tracks so what was the problem with this one?

Local Hawke's Bay Maori maintained Te Mata was their ancestor and this intrusive track had defaced the face of their ancestor. (Incidentally, 'Mata' means 'face' in Te Reo.)

In the face of vehement outrage, the winery, who had installed the track as an added attraction for their business, agreed to remove it, despite a petition of 4,000 names gathered in two days from people who wanted the track retained.

If you had been asked to sign the petition, would you?

If you had signed, would that action reflect or compromise your Christian beliefs?

The angst of local Māori could have been dismissed as superstition, but despite the loss of an attraction that would add to their income, Craggy Range Winery opted to apologise for not consulting the iwi and to remove the track – an action that would involve significant expense.

Why? The landowners decided it was important to honour Māori belief and they did not want to offend the iwi who had blessed their original business. Māori responded with joy saying, 'the mana had been restored.'

If only present day secular New Zealand took Christianity so seriously – we may wish!

As scorn is increasingly poured on Christian beliefs and rituals, Māori legends and rituals are increasingly given more respect in NZ culture. Why is this?

Despite our best efforts to show Christianity as good in the grand scheme of life, part of the blame must lie with us. A large chunk of our population, including many of our own children who were raised in our faith do not see Christianity as relevant to their lives. And it's not. Today's younger people lead very busy lives juggling study and finances or jobs and family They want leisure time and are not willing to sacrifice precious time on what they can't see as important. Young parents recognise family time as valuable but have forgotten that church values families. It is good to remind them that church is one of the few places in our society that welcomes all ages and offers a caring network.

A hook parents of Millennials hang their logic on is, 'Christians believe a lot of outmoded stuff.' Most Christians want to dispute this, but convincing others is something else. I don't think it matters much what anyone believes, as long as it is helpful to them in living well.

But if you want to pursue a meaningful discussion it is reasonable to consider that Christians are liable to fall into the trap of taking ourselves and our stories too seriously. In other words, we tend to hold inflexible views. Listening carefully and being open to modifying opinions is all important to the modern mindset.

We are ritual making creatures. Because humans have speech, humans rely on storytelling to survive, to inform, to entertain and to record.

All cultures have, and create, stories and gods. All cultures create rituals that aid emotional response. Religious rituals particularly serve to enhance respect. This should be a good thing, but to interpret ritual and symbolism as fact, is folly.

Religious beliefs are best viewed as a mix of story and poetry that help ground us in the reality of being human while recognising the divine.

One of the errors modern Christians have made is putting emphasis on explaining holy stories in a factual way rather than emphasising the spiritual significance of the story.

Consider this: both Māori and Pākehā give geographical features names that relate to shapes and people. All over the world hills, rocks or islands are called, the 12 apostles, the seven sisters, the three maidens, the chief's head, the king's seat etc. As Kiwis we are happy to accept the North Island as Te Ika-a-Māui (the Fish of Māui) and the South Island as Te Waka-a-Māui (the Canoe of Māui). Some Māori may believe that Maui was an actual physical ancestor, others may not, but all of us want respect for the earth whether we name her Papatūānuku, Mother Nature, Gaia, or God's Creation.

Questions worth considering this Lent are:

- Do our holy stories have to be factual events to have relevance?
- Have we become over invested in wanting to believe our holy stories are better than other peoples' holy stories?

The Lectionary and Liturgical Year follow a pattern. The Great Festivals of the Christian Year being Christmas, Easter and Pentecost with each relating to its special season of Advent, Christmas, Epiphany, Lent, Easter and Pentecost, followed by Ordinary Time. Lesser rituals include: Harvest Festival, Mother's Day (now 'Home and Family Sunday'), plus local festivals such as Saints Days, Spring Flower Sunday, Animal Blessings etc.

All rituals that acknowledge seasons in a spiritual way give shape and meaning to worship.

Lectionary readings also follow a prescribed pattern. Although our lectionary follows a 3-year cycle with a particular Gospel given prominence, regardless of it being year A, B, or C, after Epiphany comes the Baptism of Jesus (linked to an OT 'water story' usually Noah's Ark), followed by the Temptations, the Call of the Disciples, and then the Ministry of Jesus.

It is a natural progression. Whether we consider this spiritual journey as factual or not, is an individual choice that has little to do with our core Christian beliefs.

Consider Noah's Ark, the Bible gives five chapters to Noah and his sons, yet we hear the same few verses over and over – verses that make a delightful children's story. But the Bible wasn't written for children! The Bible is very adult and very messy. So instead of today's set lectionary reading, Genesis 9:8–17, I decided to share with you some lesser known bits of the Noah tale. Without such pieces the whole grand conservation concept would have been ruined by Noah's first act on dry land – sacrificing one of every clean animal to the Lord. Humans have always made up stories to explain important concepts.

Consider the Temptations. Matthew and Luke presume Jesus could have been tempted through hunger to use magic, power, and showmanship. In a DVD on the life of Jesus (watched at house group) the Temptation of Christ was given a modern twist. A woman in a gown of flowing scarlet was manipulated by Satan (in a business suit) to tempt Jesus. Any story of worth will be retold, and movie directors always want to showcase their creative angle on an old story. Sex tops the bill in the modern world.

It took Matthew and Luke 11 to 13 verses to describe their thoughts on what temptation was for Jesus. But Mark, the first written of the Gospels, allocates only two verses, and tells all we need to know, Jesus was tempted. We all experience temptation but we don't all experience the same temptations.

Whether you believe Māui fished up the North Island with his grandmother's jawbone or Samson slew 1,000 men with the jawbone of an ass, has very little to do with how you behave as a person. Whether you believe Māui slowed down the sun to give humans enough hours of daylight to tend their crops or that a Universal God created a sun to provide ideal light for human need, has little to do with how you behave towards your neighbours. But having respect for the sun and the earth as things of paramount importance shaped by a divine power, does affect how you behave towards our planet.

Faith is not about believing debatable facts. Faith is about living the best life you can.

Knowledge increases, every decade, every year, week and day. Known facts are replaced by further knowledge all the time and it can happen that in the rapid replacing of knowledge we lose sight of the original knowledge.

Christians, very early on, forgot that many of the Christian stories were not facts but stories told to explain and sustain spiritual belief.

In our times most of us are able to view Bible stories connected to the birth of Jesus as wonderful stories – stories that centre on a baby having the potential to change the world by appreciating the poor as well as the rich, women as well as men, and promoting peace, hope, joy and love to all – in other words 'establish the Kingdom of Christ.'

But many find it difficult to view Bible stories concerning the death and resurrection of Jesus as dramatic stories that embody the cost of standing up against corruption, and regardless of what happens, knowing working for good is always right. To live in this way and pass on this understanding is surely triumphing over evil with resurrection.

Lenten pondering has led me to conclude that:

- Everyone decides what they believe in, but some give more thought to it than others.

- All beliefs are shaped by one's own culture and personal experiences.

- Beliefs should change as we mature.

- What anyone believes is nowhere near as important as what they do.

- When it comes to living well in this world, religion is optional, but trust and respect are vital.

For myself, I trust in God and respect core values embedded in the Holy Bible, particularly those shown in the life and teaching of Jesus.

I believe: God is good; God cares; God loves; God comforts.

I trust that God is with us in the mystery and power of the Holy Spirit;

And that God wants and enables goodness to happen through us. Amen.

*[1,755 words]*

**Offertory**

In this season of struggle, we are invited to re-examine our use of the resources and abilities at our disposal.
**Our God entrusts us with unlimited opportunities and obligations.**

**Our offerings give expression of our faith and God's faithfulness.**

**Hymn:** *Will you offer me compassion?* Alleluia Aotearoa 160
(Words: John Weir. Music: Douglas Mews)

**Pastoral Prayers**

Today we will begin our time of intercession by singing the Lord's Prayer (With One Voice 676) and then we will have a time of silent prayer when we bring before God public things that weigh on our minds and personal matters that are uppermost in our hearts and conclude with the printed prayer

Dear God our hope is to:

| Fast from unkind thoughts | **May we instead feast on love,** |
| Fast from sadness | **May we feast on joy,** |
| Fast from anger | **May we feast on peace,** |
| Fast from pessimism | **May we feast on patience,** |
| Fast from discouragement | **May we feast on faithfulness,** |
| Fast from bitterness | **May we feast on kindness,** |
| Fast from negativity | **May we feast on gentleness,** |
| Fast from worry | **May we feast on goodness,** |
| Fast from indulgence | **May we feast on self-control.** |

Gracious God,

**During this season of fasting make us keenly aware of the feasting you offer.**

**Gift us with your presence, so we can be gift to others in carrying out your work. Amen.**

**Hymn:** *Come to our land, come to our hearts.* Alleluia Aotearoa 26. (Words: Shirley Erena Murray. Music: Colin Gibson)

**Commission and Blessing**

Go into the world in peace,
knowing Jesus Christ reigns in us,
**We are free to live and die with courage,**
**Trusting in God our strength,**
**And the Holy Spirit, our comfort. Amen**

# Complete Service Sample 2 — Harvest Festival

[A Special Sunday service that examples themed hymns
and prayers taken from various sources – traditional,
adapted and contemporary. The set lectionary readings
are not used in this service. The reflection is based on a
book from the Hebrew Scriptures.]

**Welcome and notices:**

**Call to worship:**

> Life is a process of growth and development,
> **We come here for nurture to keep us growing,**
>
> May our worship bring life and greening;
> **Ever ready for new possibilities**
>
> Let us worship God!

**Hymn:** *Morning has broken.* With One Voice 91.

**Harvest Prayer:**

> Abundant God,
> we meet here today in the context of a festival.
> **On this Sunday we particularly remember harvests and
> your goodness to us.**
>
> Our autumn is marked by ripe berries and plump fruit.
> We are indeed surrounded by blessings
> that grow on trees.
> **Today we give particular thanks for the bounty
> of the soil.**
>
> Because your creativity is infinite we can appreciate
> an infinite variety of food and goods.
> **Today we give particular thanks for your plenitude and
> our abundance.**

While intentionally mindful of the vital produce of farms,
orchards and gardens,
we acknowledge there are many spin off blessings
that come from living in a land of plenty.
**Today we give particular thanks that education is a
right for all our children**

Our children are not required to labour to live,
and our educated adults can choose from many work
options and creative opportunities.
**Today we give particular thanks for the many benefits
of employment.**

We have the good fortune to live in a land
of great natural beauty
that offers many pleasurable pursuits.
**Today we give particular thanks for the leisure that we
are able to enjoy.**

As we travel life's journey we encounter many people.
**Help us to find 'good and God' in all whom we meet
and wherever we go.**

**Today we give particular thanks for this church
and its people.**

Save us from becoming cynics isolated by our own
concerns or non-negotiable opinions.
**Help us to be blessing counters all the days of our lives
so we may live mindful of your continuing love now
and forever. Amen**

**Song:** *Count your blessings.* Popular 19th century chorus (Johnson
Oatman, 1897).

Count your blessings, name them one by one;
Count your blessings, see what God has done;
Count your blessings, name them one by one;
And it will surprise you what the Lord has done.

**Family time – Blessing Counting: "I spy"** (see Chapter 16 — Sample
'Family Time' slots)

**Hymn:** *We plough the fields.* Tune: Wir Pflugen, With One Voice 59
1st verse: Matthias Claudius, 1782; 2nd verse: Frank Low;
remainder adapted from original by Rosalie Sugrue.

We plough the fields, and scatter
the good seed on the land,
but it is fed and watered
by God's almighty hand.
God sends the snow in winter,
the warmth to swell the grain,
the breezes, and the sunshine,
and soft, refreshing rain.

*All good gifts around us*
*Are given by God to share,*
*Then thank the Lord, O thank our God*
*For teaching us to care.*

We now plough fields with tractors,
with drills we sow the land;
but growth is still the wondrous gift
of God's almighty hand.
We add our fertilisers
to help the growing grain;
but for its full fruition,
it needs God's sun and rain.

God is the primary maker
of all things near and far;
God paints the wayside flower,
and lights the evening star;
the winds and waves are God made,
by God the birds are fed;
and to us all is given,
far more than daily bread.

We thank you God our Parent,
for all things bright and good,
the seed time and the harvest,
our life, our health, our food.

Accept the gifts we offer
for all your love imparts,
and what you ask from us folk,
our humble, thankful hearts.

**Readings:**

Ruth 2: 17–23
Galatians. 6:1–10

**Hymn: *Come to our land.*** Alleluia Aotearoa 26.
(Words: Shirley Erena Murray. Music: Colin Gibson)

**Prayer:**

May the words of my mouth
and the meditations of our hearts
be acceptable to you O Lord,
our strength and our redeemer. Amen

**Reflection: Famine and Feast**

*'Now it came to pass in the days when the judges ruled that there was a famine in the land...'* so begins of the book of Ruth.

Mmmm ... a strange way to reflect on Harvest Festival ... shouldn't we be reflecting on abundance of food and thanksgiving?

Quite so! But our major church festivals are all Northern-centric and our Harvest time sits uncomfortably in the liturgical season of Lent and fasting. It so happens that these themes of contrast undergird the Book of Ruth.

I invite you to reflect on famine... What images come to mind...? Did you consider how it was for Biblical people or did you visualise the graphic third-world poverty seen all too frequently on our TV screens? Whether you pictured Ruth or modern images you did what sermons aim to do, relate biblical text to the here and now.

It is unlikely that anyone in this congregation has ever lived on the brink of starvation but some of you may have experienced times when feeding yourself or your family was difficult. Neither wealth nor health guarantee against occasional bouts of wretchedness. We are all prone to feeling lonely, miserable, misunderstood, lacking in worth or starved of affection. I invite you to think on such times...

Naomi, the central character of the book of Ruth, has such emotions. This woman has lost, not only her husband, whom she followed to a strange land but also both her sons. Naomi feels so bereft she says, 'call me *Mara*' – the Hebrew word for *bitter*. Her own name means *pleasant* or *sweet*. Note, Naomi did not say call me 'Hungry', soul starvation is even worse than body starvation.

Contemporary theologians tell us that the opening line of Ruth was probably not meant to be taken at face value. *There was a famine in the land,* is a good opening line for any story. The listener's attention is caught. The situation requires resolution, and thus a plot is born.

In ancient Hebrew literature '*There was a famine in the land*' equates to our '*Once upon a time.*' *Once upon a time* has no meaning apart from indicating a story will follow. *There was a famine in the land* was a way of moving characters from where they are to somewhere else, because, of course, the humdrum of ordinary life is no basis for a good story. The *Book of Ruth* is a beautiful piece of storytelling. It is a novella of four chapters. 65% of it is in dialogue. Dialogue, being in the present tense, is a literary technique that adds pace by putting the action in the now. Characters live through speech.

*Ruth* is an exceptional book in many ways and not least in being the only book in the OT without a word of condemnation for anyone. No one is horrible, and no blood is shed. Which is particularly cheering coming as it does in our canon after the *Book of Judges*. The stories in *Judges* go from bad to horrific.

In the Jewish Bible *Ruth* is placed with 'the writings' after *Proverbs*. You may recall that the last chapter of Proverbs extols '*the virtuous woman whose price is above rubies.*' Ruth may reflect these virtues.

There are only a handful of characters in the story for the audience to keep track of. The names are chosen with care. Naomi is portrayed as a pious woman and suitably, her husband's name Elimelech translates *my God is King*. Both sons' names imply *early death*. Ruth means *kind, compassionate and beautiful*. Boaz equals *strength*. Bethlehem is *house of bread*.

The story is beautifully set against a background of the *barley harvest*. Ruth is a personal tale of food, plenitude and loyalty.

*Ruth* lends itself to various interpretations. Some read it as history. Some see it as a moral tale of loyalty and generosity. Some read it as a lesbian story of unrequited love. Others read it as marginalised women driven to survive. The characters of Ruth and Naomi are praised by some theologians and condemned by others. Neither woman is as innocent or one-dimensional as Sunday School tellings have made out. But whatever the message, or the intentions of the characters, the barley harvest grounds the story. Beginning with a famine the text moves from the emptiness of Moab to the renewed fertility of Bethlehem, a good harvest, marriage and the fertility of a son.

So back to the first chapter. The first intended audience would have been shocked that any Hebrew couple would move from Bethlehem to Moab and worse, allow their sons to marry Moabite women. The origin of the Moabite people was incest. Moab and Moabites were despised. It was written in Deuteronomy that no Moabite should be admitted to the assembly of the Lord even to the 10th generation, and that no Hebrew was to promote their welfare or prosperity.

Naomi is widowed, and justly so, in the minds of the listeners. Her options are few. She decides to return home. Her daughters-in-law start to go with her, but she reminds them they have mothers of their own and the possibility of remarriage. The young women weep, kiss and cling. Orpah obeys Naomi's wish and returns to her mother's house. Ruth utters her speech of undying loyalty, to which Naomi has no response. Chapter one ends with the tantalising words. *They came to Bethlehem at the beginning of the barley harvest.*

The listeners wait expectantly and are not disappointed. Soon Ruth is gleaning in the fields behind the barley reapers. Wily Naomi had directed Ruth to the field of a kinsman without conveying this information. She also neglected to warn Ruth of the dangers of the local men. Some commentators suggest Naomi may see molestation as a way of acquiring a husband. The Bible portrays Moabites as promiscuous. Ruth arriving with Naomi could well be an embarrassment.

A more traditional view is that Naomi harboured the hope that Boaz himself would notice the good-looking young woman, as indeed he did – he warned her against the male workers and even kept a paternal eye on the foreigner, suggesting she stay near his female workers and drink from the well water drawn by his men. This snippet is a most interesting reversal of the usual Biblical male female meetings at wells. Then Boaz goes beyond the realms of common kindness, he invites her to share his own bread and wine. This was tantamount to welcoming her into his family. Ruth kept some of the food offered her to take home to Naomi. True to her promise Ruth always remains loyal to Naomi. After the meal Boaz instructed his reapers to leave larger than usual gleanings for the foreign woman.

Naomi is astounded by the pickings Ruth brings home. Delighted, she discloses to Ruth that Boaz is a kinsman and proceeds to give the warning she should have given earlier. Chapter two ends with these words – 'so she stayed close to the young women of Boaz, gleaning until the end of the barley and wheat harvest; and she lived with her mother-in-law.'

Some Bibles title chapter three *Ruth and Boaz at the Threshing Floor*. Hosea 9:1 is explicit about threshing floors but you don't have to be a keen Bible scholar to pick up on the suggestion. In English folklore reference to haystacks, hayrides and haylofts give the same implication. Naomi masterminds a plan and it seems Ruth is a willing participant. She certainly plays her part well.

Why does the respectable landlord take notice of the Moabitess? Was Boaz a particularly generous landowner? Did he feel obliged to help his widowed kinswoman? This was a legal Hebrew requirement. But when Ruth makes advances on the threshing floor his focus is not the elder widow. We can presume Boaz was middle-aged, we know he was flattered. He commends Ruth for not going after the younger men and spreads his cloak over her.

After the threshing floor incident Ruth is no longer described as *foreigner, servant* or *handmaiden*. Boaz calls her a *worthy woman*. Naomi calls her *daughter* and the narrator calls her *woman*. Later she is described as both the *wife* and *widow of Mahlon*. Although her status has been raised she is still *Ruth the Moabite*.

To marry a Moabitess is not something to be taken lightly, and in the manner of novels, Boaz finds a way to make it Ok. Adding new dramatic interest, is the intrigue of the land deal. Elimelech owned a field that Naomi is entitled to sell. Only in exceptional circumstances could women own land, and there was the proviso that such land remained in the husband's family.

The audience hears of a relative closer than Boaz, presumably not as attractive, but a decent man who was willing to buy the field. Willing until he finds it has a condition attached, a clever condition, imposed by Boaz. With the land parcel came the foreign woman. The close relative had no wish to marry a Moabitess and so forfeited his claim. Thus, Boaz was able to legally acquire both the field and the woman.

The women of the town are generous in their good wishes. Their blessings make references to Leah and Rachael (we know a fair bit of skulduggery went on in that household) and they express the hope that Ruth will be as Tamar. This could be a fertility wish as Tamar bore twins but only the elder twin is mentioned. Tamar's twins were the result of seduction and trickery. The text implies that the women understood what had happened and they approved. And naturally, the harvest-hints of fertility come to pass. Blessed by God, Boaz and Ruth produce a child, whom the women declare as 'a child born to Naomi.'

The final genealogy spells out the punch line of the story. Baby Obed becomes the father of Jesse, who is the father of David. The child of the Moabitess is destined to be the grandfather of King David. The greatest of Israel's kings was not of pure blood!

Set against the barley harvest, the *Book of Ruth* carries premonition of David's reign being blessed with fertility and plenitude.

But what message could this story hold for us? It could be saying famine need not persist. We can resolve to take action. We are reminded of the circular nature of seasons. The seasons background life. There is toil in the planting, tending and the gathering but the harvest comes. The gathered harvest is cause for celebration. The book of Ruth is a testament to loyalty and generosity but also to initiative and compromise.

We do well to look at the story of Ruth and ask ourselves who are my Moabites? Then we need to move from the famine in our lives.

God creates all people. God loves all people. I believe if we accept this truth as significant to our way of being we are enabled to fully appreciate the bounty of the harvest, or as Paul puts it in Galatians 6:9

'So let us not grow weary in doing what is right, for we will reap at harvest time, if we do not give up.' Amen.

*[1,865 words]*

*Sources:*
*Notes from lectures given by Rev Judith McKinlay;*
*The Women's Bible Commentary, edited by C A, Newson & S H Ringe*

**Offertory:** (Said together)

> **We give Thee but Thine own,**
> **Whate'er the gift may be;**
> **All that we have is Thine alone,**
> **A trust, O Lord, from Thee. Amen**

*(William W How, 1854)*

**Pastoral Prayers:**

> God of Goodness,
> We acknowledge that we
> are particularly fortunate to live
> in this land of Aotearoa:
>
> A country of mild climate, rich soils,
> and abundant fresh water;
> A country of natural beauty, with space
> for all its citizens to live in harmony.
> A country surrounded by protective seas,
> and governed by thoughtful, caring people.
>
> In Aotearoa all people can move freely
> without encountering dangerous wild creatures,
> armed militias, or officials demanding bribes.
> Our country has no divisive land borders
> or intimidating check-points;
> We have the benefits of responsible government
> that provides universal education and welfare,
> and promotes respect for all persons.
> We are profoundly grateful.
>
> We also acknowledge this is not how it is
> for many countries and many millions of people.

This saddens us, and we presume to think
saddens you; your infinite love entwined with grief
as you watch evils perpetuated by your people.
As we understand it, limiting the free will
of human beings was never your way.

But we believe you can be with all people,
at all times, comforting and inspiring goodness.

Our earnest request and hope
is that our prayers of good intention
can be used in your service
helping you, in what you do. Amen.

**Hymn:** *Our life has its seasons.* Alleluia Aotearoa, 113.
(Words: Shirley Erena Murray. Music: Colin Gibson)

**Benediction:** *said together*

**God**

**is**

**if**

**we**

**but look and see**

**and open hearts to reality**

**colour and vigour mark our lent**

**recalling Christ his life well spent**

**with freezers full the harvest is ours**

**God flings fruit on top of flowers**

**feel the Spirit rushing free**

**see God in leaves blown**

**from painted tree**

**think on God**

**and be**

**Sung Amen:**

# 16 — Sample 'Family Time' slots

'Family Time' replaces the regular 'children's talk' in a traditional service. The beauty of such a slot is that children across a range of ages can be catered for in a way that engages adults regardless of the presence of children by seeking active participation by all.

## New Year (Expect to find solutions to things that seem impossible)

Comment that each New Year brings new experiences, new delights and new problems. Some things may seem impossible but don't give up searching for new ways to achieve the seemingly impossible.

Produce a birthday card and a small pair of scissors. Ask the congregation what they do with their old birthday cards. Explain that you like to do creative things with yours like making jigsaws or murals and just having fun with them up. If school children are present, ask for a volunteer or volunteers (you will need to have a card and scissors for each). Say: "If I give you a card could you cut a hole in it big enough for you to put your foot through? Do you think that is possible?" The children may say it can't be done others may want to try and will quickly discover they can't make a big enough hole.

Say: "Things that may look impossible may not be. I can cut a hole in this card that you will be able to put your foot through. If there was enough time I could make a hole in this card big enough for you to climb right through. Watch me!" Describe what you are doing.

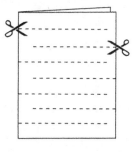

Make a cut in a card starting at the folded edge and stopping about a centimetre before the open edges. Turn and make a parallel cut stopping about 1 cm before the folded edge. Continue until all the card has been evenly cut, making sure the last cut begins at the fold. Then open the card and cut along the folded edge making sure the first and last folds remain intact, and gently pull the two ends apart. The size of the hole depends on the width between the cuts. It is easy to make a gap that will stretch over a child, but you don't want them getting bored by the process, so go for wider cuts that quickly enable a child to pull up over one leg. (*Without practise the trick is likely to go wrong. You also need to get a feel for the approximate width and number of cuts required.*) You may like to finish by producing a prepared narrow slit card for a child step through.

If you have enough scissors, distribute them with cards, among all the children to try it for themselves with parental guidance. If no children are present, you can still ask for a volunteer. If none are forthcoming do it using yourself as the volunteer.

## Harvest Festival (I spy)

Comment on the attractiveness of the harvest display then proceed to play 'I spy' with the whole congregation, focussing on the harvest produce. Ask why we have a harvest festival? Follow up with words along the lines of: we are blessed to have such a wonderful variety of things to eat but we are blessed with many good things and some of the best things are not things we can spy with our eyes. Some of the best things are felt more than seen. We feel things not with our seeing eyes but with what can be called our 'inner eye.' We are now going to play a different version of I spy. In this game instead of saying, I spy with my little eye' we say, 'I spy with my inner eye.' I'm thinking of something (an abstract noun) that Jesus told us is very important: 'I spy with my inner eye something beginning with L.' After getting Love, others will follow up with K (Kindness), B (Beauty), C (Caring) etc. An extra clue is given along with the letter.

## Lent (What's missing?)

Make a physical impact in a Lenten service by asking that there are no flowers, and remove or cover banners where possible along with special items including things normally on the Communion Table such as a small cross, candle, chalice and paten etc.

Comment on Lent being a time of reflection and for some a time of denial. Explain how Anglican and Catholic churches emphasise these attributes by altering the appearance of their worship space. Ask what is missing from our church today. Then ask for detailed descriptions on the items, particularly banners and any words on the banners. Remind that we are all in danger of taking things (and people) for granted when they are always there. Encourage the congregation to be more attentive in looking carefully at the special things (and people) that help us in our worship (and in our life). Search for deeper meaning carried by the symbolic furnishings in our church (and deeper appreciation of people of the people in our lives).

## Hiroshima Day

Tell the story of Sadako Sasaki, the Japanese girl who folded paper cranes for peace before dying of leukaemia caused by the atomic bomb dropped on Hiroshima on 6 August 1945.

Japanese tradition says that if one creates a thousand cranes, they are granted one wish. Sadako's wish was to have a world without nuclear weapons. Thousands of origami cranes from all over the world are offered around the monument. If PowerPoint is available show a photo of the Children's Peace Monument that features her. Throughout the service have one or more people, who know how, folding paper cranes and give one to each person present at the end of the service. Supply printed instructions for the children (or anyone) to take home with them.

## All good ideas can be adapted to fit different situations

Although I have assigned particular Sundays to the above samples they can be adapted for other Sundays. With any visual aid you can adapt the words you use to suit the age range of the congregation.

### *Rhyming Stories*

If reading a rhyming story intended for young children and older children are present, don't say the word that rhymes. Invite the older children to call out the rhyming word.

### *Presenting parables*

If a parable features in the lectionary for the day, instead of having the Bible passage read, try telling the story and invite volunteers to be characters and come up with their own dialogue. This only works for parables that have interacting characters. Some parables are suitable for children to illustrate with actions. As you describe what is taking place volunteers mime the action, e.g. The Sower and the Seeds; The Houses Built on Sand and Rock; The Lost Coin; The Lost Sheep.

# Doing and things – creative child participation

For example, survival by cooperation.

Don't introduce the subject as such. Make up a fantasy story about two groups of people having a spell cast on them by a witch (or by any other means that made them unable to bend their elbows). The two groups are in separate rooms. The rooms have tables and chairs, bottles of water, a basket of bananas and a stack of books and games. The only way to break the spell is for each person in the room to eat a banana. At the end of the day the witch returned to find a heap of banana skins and a happy group of people in one room and in the other room a group of hungry people with sore, stiff arms.

Ask: If you had been one of those people what would you have done? Tell the volunteers they must keep their arms straight and to pick up a banana and eat it. Let them experiment. If they can't work out a solution, suggest that cooperation is the best way to solve any problem especially when it concerns food distribution. (*Work together in pairs to peel a banana and feed each other.*)

### Sin or the danger of getting into bad habits
This can be illustrated by winding a strand of cotton around a child's wrists explaining, one little lie or doing one bad thing, might not cause much harm. Pretend this cotton is one little lie. Can you snap the cotton? But, if you keep telling lies or doing bad things you will cause a lot of harm to others and you may not be able to break the habit of doing bad things. (Wind the cotton round the wrists several times.) Can you snap the cotton now? A time will come when you won't be able to get out of trouble without help. It is lucky that I have some scissors.

## Background Information

### Symbols and History
It is surprising how little most regular pew sitters know about the background of Christian traditions and they are interested in finding out.

I explain the meanings behind Christian symbols by showing a picture and having the congregation give suggestions as to what the symbol may mean or how it may have originated. Symbols for the

Gospel writers and the 'sign of the fish' lend themselves to unpacking in this way. Other symbols such as the World Day of Prayer, or the Fellowship of the Least Coin and Good News Bible logo can be illustrated by posing people to replicate what is being symbolised.

The peace sign is fun to explore by considering semaphore. (Some who were in Guides or Scouts may remember how the alphabet is formed and be able to demonstrate N and D). The peace symbol was designed in 1958 by British artist Gerald Holtom for the Campaign for Nuclear Disarmament and represents the semaphore letters N and D.

The children may enjoy learning the word RUN – both arms stretched out sideways for R, up angled out for U, down angled out for N. D is formed with right arm straight up, left arm straight down.

### *Names for church furnishings*

These can be taught by handing out cards labelled: Pulpit, Lectern, Communion table, chalice, paten, Amnesty International candle etc. Encourage the children to work together to try and read the words. Praise good attempts and give help as needed. Then ask them to take turns at placing a card on or by the object. If the child does not know what or where the object is, tell the child to take three steps in any direction. The congregation directs further steps by saying: "getting hotter" (right direction) or "colder" (wrong direction). Older children may enjoy a spelling competition to consolidate what they have learnt.

### *Liturgical Colours*

Explain how the seasons of the Church Calendar and special celebrations have an assigned liturgical colour that is used for preaching stoles, altar cloths, pulpit falls and Bible bookmarks. Name the colours (violet, white, red, green) and invite season suggestions; or name the seasons (information in the lectionary) and invite colour suggestions: (**violet:** preparation – Advent, Lent; **white:** light, joy – Christmas, Easter, Baptism, Weddings; **red:** fire, Pentecost, ordination, induction; **green:** growth, used during 'ordinary time' from Pentecost to Advent).

Activity: Make bookmarks from prepared oblongs of white card; colour a border and draw an appropriate symbol for the season or celebration.

### Stories

Picture books can be presented as a PowerPoint display, but younger children tend to lose interest. Telling stories is one of the best ways to engage an audience. Good story tellers do not need any props they capture attention by voice alone. I find simple props useful but not essential. Too many props can cause complications that destroy the flow.

You need to be very familiar with a story before you can tell it. Read it several times silently and at least once out loud. Prepare a few headings that you could glance at should the need arise. If using props, you need to practise, ideally with an audience (*family or spouse can be useful critics*).

### Other Symbols

World Day
of Prayer

Fellowship of
the Least Coin

Fish / ICHTHYS
**An early Christian
symbol, which in Greek
was code for *Jesus Christ,
God's Son, Saviour***

# 17 — Sample Cafe Services

('Cafe' meaning sitting in a circle or at tables with
refreshments either provided during the service or to follow)

## Sample Cafe Service 1
## Spirit of Creation – Tree Sunday

**Things to prepare**

Set of 10 cards with printed Bible verses.

Copy the verses from the Bible Gateway website, paste them to an A4
folder and adjust font and spacing before printing. For cardboard I
cut cereal boxes into strips, staple the printed text to the shiny side,
write the reference number on back. Only print the Bible text, added
words are for your information.

**Bible verses**

| | | |
|---|---|---|
| 1. Genesis 3:6 | Eve & Adam | 1. The Tree of Knowledge. |
| 2. Genesis 6:14 | Noah | 2. Cypress [or gopher] wood. |
| 3. Genesis 13:18 | Abraham | 3. The Oaks of Mamre. |
| 4. Judges 4:4–5 | Deborah | 4. The Palm of Deborah. |
| 5. Judges 9:8 | Jotham | 5. The Parable of the Trees. |
| 6. 1 Kings 19:4–5 | Elijah | 6. A broom [or juniper] tree. |
| 7. 1 Kings 5:10 | King Hiram of Lebanon | 7. Timber of cedar and cypress. |
| 8. Jonah 4:6 | Jonah | 8. A gourd vine [or bush]. |
| 9. Matthew 13:31–32 | Jesus | 9. A mustard tree. |
| 10. Luke 19:3–5 | Zacchaeus | 10. A sycamore tree. |

**Poster and art materials**

On poster sized paper draw the outline of your forearm tracing from
below the elbow around spread fingers pointing up. Colour the shape
grey/brown or cut it from contrasting paper and glue into position.
Along the bottom of the poster print GIVE WITHOUT SEEKING
ANY REWARD.

**Things to gather**

A selection of pages torn from magazines containing photos of people. Make a few cardboard stencils with leaf-shaped centres sized to surround a face in the photos. Also required: scissors, pens and glue-sticks.

**Before the service**

Find a volunteer to read the poem. Set up the art table. Distribute the text cards around the other tables placed face down. Ask the people to not turn them over.

**Welcome & Notices:**

**Call to worship:** (*said together*)

> **In the presence of the faithful**
> **I will proclaim your name, for it is good.**
>
> **I am like a green olive tree**
> **in the house of God.**
> **I trust in the steadfast love of God**
> **forever and ever.**
>
> **We will thank you forever,**
> **because of what you have done.**

*(from Psalm 52)*

**Hymn:** *All people that on earth do dwell.* With One Voice 10.

**Prayer for our Earth:**

> Loving God:
>
> **We pray that we, and all people,**
> **may increasingly work together**
> **to establish your reign upon earth;**
>
> We pray that the world's resources
> can be gathered, distributed, and used
> **with unselfish motives and scientific skill,**
> **for the greatest benefit of all,**
> **and always with care for the earth itself.**

May planned beauty be given to our cities,
and natural left to our countryside.
**May open ways, and freedom be
enjoyed by all cultures and creatures**.

Your essence and title is 'Good.'
Help us to recognise all that is good:

**The good earth you made
and the divine spirit you planted in each of us.
Help us cherish the world you created.
Help us value the good that is in all creation
and the God that is in all people
by the grace of your holy Spirit.** *Amen*

*(Introduce the theme with a poem, read by the prepared volunteer)*

**Poem:** *Trees.* Joyce Kilmer (1914)

I think that I shall never see
A poem lovely as a tree.

A tree whose hungry mouth is prest
Against the earth's sweet flowing breast;

A tree that looks at God all day,
And lifts her leafy arms to pray;

A tree that may in Summer wear
A nest of robins in her hair;

Upon whose bosom snow has lain;
Who intimately lives with rain.

Poems are made by fools like me,
But only God can make a tree.

**Family Time**

Invite the children to come the centre of the circle for a chat time. (*A large mat provides sitting space.*) We are thinking about trees today. Do you have a favourite tree? How many different trees can you think of? Let's hear some tree names... (*In these chats the adults join in when the children need prompting or have run out of ideas.*)

## What can trees do?

Trees give:
Food (fruit, nuts, maple syrup); shelter (shade, timber); beauty (form, flowers).

Trees help the environment:
provide shade, homes for insects and birds; take in carbon give out oxygen; filter ground water; stop slips and erosion, form boundaries and shelter-belt.

## What can you do with trees?

Climb, swing, hide, hug, make tree huts, stumps make seats.

Conclude with something along these lines... Trees certainly do many useful things and they don't ask for any reward. Do trees have hands? They do have branches, does anyone know another name for branches – it is a word that can also mean arms and legs? Some people are a bit like trees because they do useful things without asking for any reward. People are lucky to not only have limbs but fingers to help them do good things.

## Poster activity

Show the prepared poster and explain the task, turning the arm into a people tree by adding leaves made from faces. Direct the children to a table or floor space where the art materials are set out and explain how to position a stencil over a face, draw around the stencil, and cut out the shapes to use as leaves by pasting them around the fingers.

## Adult Activity:

**Discussion:** Tree stories from the Bible.

* What trees are named in the Bible?

* Can you think of any stories that mention trees?

* Let's match up some Bible characters with trees – any suggestions?

Give clues by naming characters, or trees, from the list. As characters are matched, or not, call out the card number that relates to the incident for someone at the table with that number to verify by reading the Bible passage

**Hymn:** *All things bright and beautiful.* With One Voice 70.
(With added verse by Rosalie Sugrue)

> God gave us minds to think with,
> And this we want to share –
> O please be wise and thrifty
> And for our planet care.

**Readings:**

> Judges 9:7–14
> Revelation 22:1–2

**Reflection: The Tree of Life**

The Bible narrative is framed by trees. Trees are mentioned in the first chapter of Genesis and the last chapter of Revelation. There are many mentions of trees within the bible. They are mentioned in different ways, some practical such as defining location or providing timber or as part of an incident and referred to in poetical ways as in Psalms and the Song of Solomon. But they are also used in allegorical and mythological ways as in parables and folk-stories. The meaning may not be clear, but such stories invite us to ponder important concepts.

As we know there are many kinds of trees and all are beautiful in their own way. Trees have many functions, some more specific to a particular type of tree – such as providing: food, timber, shelter; or supporting the ecosystem by hosting living creatures, preventing erosion, filtering ground water and acting as lungs to the environment. Some trees are mainly ornamental and others capable of many functions, but even trees that don't appear to have an obvious function have some God given purpose to fulfil.

Creative and unlikely purposes – fig leaves for clothes – Adam & Eve (Genesis 3:7)

Capable of good but also harm – can crush and kill – Absalom (2 Samuel 18:9)

We are like trees – each of us is different, all with potential, capable of causing harm and doing good, some more useful than others, but all things of beauty with a purpose to fulfil.

Trees were important to Jesus. As a carpenter wood provided his livelihood but he also appreciated living trees for the food, shelter

107

and beauty they provided. He spoke eloquently of them in parables such as the mustard seed 'that grows to a tree that puts forth large branches, so that the birds of the air can make nests in its shade.'

The *Tree of Life* is the first named tree in the Bible and also the last-named tree. It is an allegorical tree and as such lends itself to various interpretations. Some suggesting that to eat of this tree bestows immortality (as in the myth of Lilith*). In Bible text it is used in the context of 'paradise' – Eden and Heaven. The *Tree of Life* is further described in the book of Proverbs, seen as a feminine and those who hold her fast to her are called happy (3:18). The fruit of the righteous is a *tree of life*, but violence takes lives away (11:6). Hope deferred makes the heart sick, but a desire fulfilled is a *tree of life* (13:12). A gentle tongue is a *tree of life (15:4).*

Like trees we have a God given purpose. Between us are many different abilities that we fulfil best by *being what we are meant to be.*

*By doing what we are meant to do* we are life givers – happy in holding fast to goodness, rejecting violence, gentle of tongue and bringers of healing. The *Tree of Life* will be immortal for as long as humans are willing to be its leaves.

Invite the children show their 'human' Tree of Life poster.

> * Lilith was the mythical first wife of Adam created before him. She ate from both trees before waking the sleeping red earth man. Being knowledgeable she wanted equal rights. When not granted this by the man the winged woman flew away. Being immortal she still exists. Men have portrayed her as a she devil but some women's groups revere her as the prime feminist. She is referred to in Isaiah 34:14. The KJV says: "…the 'screech owl' also shall rest here, and find for herself a place of rest." The NRSV uses the more accurate translation 'Lilith.'

**Offering:**

Creator God we ask for your blessing.

**We often feel insignificant, but we know
you seeded each of us with divine potential.
Help us nurture ourselves and each other
so we may grow to be the people you intended.**

Bless what we bring and what we give.
May these offerings and our lives
be well used in serving you. Amen

**Pastoral Prayers:**

*Concluding with...*

Creator God we give you thanks
for the world you created,
A world of wonder and infinite diversity,
Our desire is to respect your creation
and to delight in your goodness.
Show us how to be wise stewards,
Forgive us for past wrongs,
and lead us to better ways.

Help us to:
Listen carefully,
Research diligently,
Think carefully,
Plan wisely,
Act with sensitivity.
And may the peace of God disturb us always. Amen

**Song:** *Touch the earth lightly.* Alleluia Aotearoa 143.
(Words: Shirley Erena Murray. Music: Colin Gibson)

**The Grace:** (*said with congregation holding hands*)

# Sample Cafe Service 2

**Preparation**

Construct a 'pop-up well' from a large cardboard carton. Find a brown cardboard carton that can fold flat; fold the bottom flaps to interlock for a firm base and fold the top flaps down inside the carton to make a hole. A can of brown spray paint is the best way to add the effect of stones or bricks, but lines drawn with black vivid marker give the idea. Make a lid from a smaller carton by folding it flat and keeping it flat with tape or staples. Draw the silhouette of a water jar and cut out five jar shapes. Fit one with a base or prop that allows it to stand on the lid of the well.

Not essential but nice: five long flimsy scarves of different colours for the women to drape over their heads (they are cheap to buy in 'Good as Gold' type shops). If you can get a red scarf, give it to the Samaritan woman).

**Greetings & Notices:**

**Call to worship:**

> Kia ora tātou!
> **Kia ora!**

> The works of the Creator are visible;
> **The example of Jesus is apparent;**

> Let us worship in spirit and truth;
> **We come to worship God.**

**Hymn:** *In this familiar place.* Alleluia Aotearoa 72

**Prayer of Approach:**

> Eternal God we know you are everywhere,
> But this familiar building is especially sacred
> to this congregation.
> **Here we find the supportive company of**
> **current Christian travellers.**
> **We offer thanks for our church home and**
> **thanks for our companions.**

110

On this special day of prayer help us
centre in the reality of your love
as we reflect on our lives and our place
in this corner of your world.
**We respect the traditions from which we have come,**
**Help us build on those traditions**
**a strong faith for now.**
**We respect your holy word as found**
**in the sacred scriptures.**
**Help us understand its implications for our time.**

God of Moses and Miriam,
God of Mary and Jesus,
**To you, loving God of all**
**We open our hearts and minds. Amen.**

## Family Time: Wells

Imagine a well... what came into to your mind? Was it: Jack and Jill... an ornamental wishing well... a rustic well in a parched Third World country?

Has anyone here ever drawn water from a well? Has anyone stayed in house that didn't have indoor plumbing? Who has slept in a tent? Did your tent have a water tap? How did you manage to wash and cook? (Briefly share with neighbour). *Organise children to draw pictures of wells.*

We so take taps for granted but it's only 100 or so years ago since indoor plumbing became available to ordinary folk, the likes of us. In the Bible, rivers and lakes are revered and wells get frequent mention. Today we are going to reflect on one of these water stories.

## Readings:

Water from the Rock – Exodus 17:1–7
The Woman of Samaria – John 4:1–30 *(3 voices)*

## Chorus: *Never thirst again*

**We are feeding on the living Bread,**
**We are drinking at the Fountain head;**
**And whoso drinketh, Jesus said,**
**Shall never, never thirst again.**

(Women) *What! never thirst again?*
(Men) **No, never thirst again!**
(Women) *What! never thirst again?*
(Men) **No, never thirst again!**

**And whoso drinketh, Jesus said,**
**Shall never, never thirst again.**

## Play reading

Explain we are doing an unrehearsed play reading and hand out scripts and headscarves. (You may feel more at ease if you pre-select the main character and email her the script). Highlight the individual parts so each character can easily see when she speaks.

Produce the pop-up well with the jar standing on the lid and hand out the other jars. Have the well one side of the 'stage area' and the women the other.

**Introduce the play and characters:**

### Go and Tell
A reflection on the Woman of Samaria, John 4:4–43
By Rosalie Sugrue,

Cast and personalities, ladies please bow when your character is introduced:

**Leah** – a natural leader.
**Lois** – curious by nature.
**Ruth** – tends to be judgemental.
**Lydia** – an observant woman.
**The Woman of Samaria (WoS)** – draw your own conclusions.

Scene:     It is dusk. Four Eastern women carrying water jars are walking towards a well.

Leah:     Someone has left their water jar here.

(*All move closer and group around the well, facing the front, Lois looks in the jar*)

Lois:     It hasn't even been filled.

Ruth:     How careless!

Lydia:     Why would anyone leave their jar at the well?

| | |
|---|---|
| Leah: | It is a mystery, but we better get on with the job. I wish this lid wasn't so heavy. |
| Lois: | Look who's coming! |
| Ruth: | The brazen hussy! How dare she come at this time! The mid-day heat is all she's fit for. |
| Lydia: | She knows respectable women don't mix with her type. |
| WoS: | Good evening ladies. I've come to get my jar. (*The women turn away muttering similar statements to the above*) |
| WoS: | I know you don't expect to see me here ... but wouldn't you like to know why my water jar is here? |
| Ruth: | If you couldn't get the lid off by yourself, don't expect us to help you. |
| WoS: | I can manage this lid on my own. I do it every day. |
| Lois: | Well, why is your empty jar here? |
| WoS: | I've had the most amazing experience. When I arrived at my usual time there was a man here and he asked me to give him a drink. |
| Lydia: | You always were the obliging sort when it comes to men. |
| WoS: | Even though we played together as children, you don't know me at all. This man wasn't a Samaritan, but he knew who I was, not my name, but who I really am. |
| Ruth: | Your reputation sure has spread! |
| WoS: | I know what you think Ruth. And you are so wrong. He was a decent man and a Jew. |
| Leah: | But Samaritans don't have dealings with Jews. |
| WoS: | That's what I said, Leah. I was very surprised that he even spoke to me. Then I noticed he didn't have anything to draw water with and I thought he must be really thirsty. But no, he wasn't thirsty. He said he had water, special water, 'living water' he called it. He said whoever drinks this water would never be thirsty again. And then I realised he was a prophet. |

| | |
|---|---|
| Ruth: | (*sarcastically*) You looked into his eyes, deeply, I imagine. |
| WoS: | Yes, Ruth, I did. And I saw something I have not seen in a long while, I saw compassion. But it was unsettling ... the man said I should go and get my husband. My heart thudded but his eyes were so kind I held my gaze and I told him plainly I don't have a husband. But, this man knew that I was not living with my husband! |
| Lois: | We all know that. |
| WoS: | He not only knew, he understood why. I am not ashamed of my life. |
| Lydia: | Tell us more ... please. |
| WoS: | Looking into those eyes I knew I was drinking that 'living water' and it was filling my body with joy. I had no need to ashamed. We talked about my first husband dying leaving two children, me marrying his brother and having four small children when he died and how I had another to the uncle who wanted a son but didn't want me. |
| Lydia: | Caring for five children without a man would be hard. |
| WoS: | He understood how hard. After all my close relations had died there was a man who said I could live with him. What he wanted didn't include the inconvenience of children. |
| Leah: | I'm sorry we were so quick to judge. (*Others nod and murmur reluctant agreement*) |
| WoS: | Now, having met the prophet I feel free – free to be the person I really am – a loving and a confident woman. When the prophet's friends arrived with food they were surprised to see me having this deep conversation with their leader. But he kept talking to me. |
| Ruth: | Remarkable! |

| | |
|---|---|
| WoS | He said it didn't matter if people worshiped God on this sacred mountain or in the holy city of Jerusalem. He said the important thing is to worship God in Spirit and in truth. I understood what he meant. It was a revelation, an epiphany! It came to me that he might be the promised one, the messiah. |

*(Ruth and Lois roll their eyes and shake their heads disparagingly)*

| | |
|---|---|
| Leah: | So, why did you leave your water jar? |
| WoS: | Well, and this is amazing, He said, 'Go and tell.' Immediately I felt I had to share this source of 'living water' with others. So, I rushed to the city gate where the men were sitting in the shade of the wall as they do in the middle of the day. I felt so different and confident that I was able to speak to them and convince them to see this man for themselves. |
| Lois: | I heard my Samuel talking about this man to our neighbour Dan. He said there is a prophet in town who is speaking in the market place tomorrow. |
| Ruth: | Who would have thought a woman would be listened to by men? |
| WoS: | The men did listen and then they went and saw for themselves. |
| Lydia: | That is truly amazing. |
| WoS: | The man I met, right here at this well has changed my life forever. |
| Lois: | Could he change ours? |
| WoS: | He already has. You haven't spoken to me in years. Few women have. It's like I don't have a name. But I haven't forgotten your names. And what's more I believe I have been chosen by God to talk to you – Leah, Lois, Lydia and Ruth. |
| Leah: | You are a strange person for God to choose. But the Holy Stories often speak of God choosing unlikely people. Our Father Jacob did some dubious things, yet God used him mightily. What do you think God wants you to proclaim? |

| | |
|---|---|
| WoS: | Just this: God loves everyone regardless of who they are, what they are, or what they have done. God understands everything and is always with you. You don't have to be important to tell this news. You just have to share your story. |
| Lydia: | Your story is amazing. I wouldn't be surprised if you are remembered for a very long time, even if your name isn't. |
| Lois: | Are all lives important? |
| WoS: | They are ... I'm sure of it! When I looked into the prophet's eyes I could see he loved me – not in a man woman way – but in the way we love our children. Don't you love each one of your children? Even when they do things you don't like you still love them. You can't protect your children from everything or give them everything they want, but you keep on loving them. |
| Leah: | Listening to others and hearing their stories can be life changing. |
| WoS: | The 'living water' of God's compassion is for everyone. |
| Lois: | But how can everyone know this? |
| Lydia: | We can't tell everyone, but we can share what we know with people we meet. |
| Ruth: | Working together would make it easier. |
| Leah: | Let's get the lid off this well.<br>(*All working together lift the lid and draw water, to background music of 'Go, tell it on the mountain...*) |

**All sing: *Go tell it on the mountain* (adapted)**

Go tell it on the mountain
Over the hills and everywhere
Go tell it on the mountain
That Jesus Christ has come.

Come, share the living water
And give nourishment to all
Take pride in what you all do
Help everyone stand tall.

**Reflection:** *Living Water*

To understand the importance of water in the Bible we need to feel into what it was like to live in a dry land. In the Middle East, water is scarce and precious. In Israel the rain only falls in two short rainy seasons. Most town dwellers survived by sinking deep wells or using stagnant water that was stored in cisterns. When the rain fell again after months of clear skies, it felt like a miraculous gift from God

Within hours the hills change from a barren brown to a green fuzz and within days meadows of grass and flowers appear. But soon after the rain stops the lush vegetation withers to mere strips lining the river banks, and only yards away, all is barren.

The River Jordan that flows from the Lake of Galilee rushes down the Promised Land to pour into another lake, a lake that looks stunning, but cannot be drunk because this lake is full of poisonous salts. The fresh water that arrived at this lake has nowhere to go and here it stops and turns deadly.

Israelites understood the importance of flowing water. They also knew that deep wells provided safe drinking water and may have had a concept of underground rivers. They believed water had a Spiritual significance. Not only did it support life, to them it was both a sign of God, and a symbol for God. Jeremiah uses the words "Living Water" to describe God.

We too, understand that water is more than a life-giving necessity, water nourishes the soul. Be it a tumbling stream, gentle lake, rolling river or mighty ocean, water has the power to inspire and uplift the viewer. Be it surrounded by native bush, wild flowers, mowed grass, rocks or sand, water invites us to contemplate the Divine and be renewed by its presence. The concept of living water invigorates our being, refreshing us to live in goodness and in God.

**Offering Dedication**

**Pastoral Prayers:**
*(Given by the rostered member of congregation, concluding with the Lord's Prayer)*

**Hymn:** *Let justice roll down like a river.* Alleluia Aotearoa 85.
(Words and music: Colin Gibson)

**Benediction/Commission:**

As a pool invites contemplation,
**We go reflecting on our faith;**

As a well gives water to nurture life,
**We go enlivened by Christ's living water;**

As a river rolls down to the sea,
**We go to be agents of peace and justice.**

**Sing:** *The Edelweiss Blessing*

May our faithful, loving God
bless and keep you forever.
Grant you peace, grace and strength,
courage in every endeavour.
Lift your eyes to see God's face
and know that grace forever.
May our steadfast, loving God
bless and keep you forever.

# 18 — Ideas for Devotions, Family Time and Less Formal Services

## Advent Kindness Calendar

An Advent Calendar with 24 pockets is required. Handcrafted fabric Advent Calendars with treat pockets are popular in some European countries. However, such an item can be replicated by machine stitching wide ribbon in rows across a small, cheap Christmas tablecloth. Stitch the wide ribbon (fabric or paper) along the bottom edge in spaced rows. Create 24 pockets by stitching evenly spaced rows from top to bottom across the rows of ribbon. Number the pockets with a vivid marker. Turn and stitch along the top edge of the cloth so a rod or stick can be inserted to hold it like a banner.

Print the advent kindness suggestions (see below), cut into narrow strips, fold and place one in each pocket. Put extras in some pockets if there is likely to be more than 24 people.

Invite everyone to choose a number and extract a kindness slip.

In pairs share and discuss:

- Have you ever received this kindness?

- Would you be able to give this kindness this Advent?

- If less than 20 people you may have time for everyone to read out their slip and swap slips, so everyone has something they can commit to doing this Advent.

| | |
|---|---|
| Send a handwritten letter this Christmas | Make creative cards for some special people. |
| Gift wrap home-made biscuits or sweets, to show appreciation. | Give someone a hug and tell them why they are special. |
| Show particular gratitude to a family member you may take for granted. | Offer to babysit for a busy mum or visit someone who can't get out. |
| Go out of the way to offer someone a ride. | Arrange to take someone to the movies. |
| Take a surprise afternoon tea to volunteers. | Give money or a Christmas gift to a homeless person. |
| Introduce yourself to a neighbour you don't know. | Arrange a lunch out with someone who lives alone. |
| Host a gathering of neighbours. | Share a Christmas recipe. |
| Teach someone a skill or share a hobby over the holiday period. | Offer to take a photo for someone taking a family group photo |
| Praise a shop assistant or tradesperson. | Offer to pay for someone having trouble finding change. |
| Let someone with small children go ahead of you in a queue. | Get, or return, a supermarket trolley for a person with mobility problems. |
| Take someone cut flowers from your garden or make a Christmas posy. | Treat someone a tea or coffee when out or invite a neighbour to your house. |
| Lend someone a book you've enjoyed with a view to discussing it when read. | Make a point of complimenting someone every day throughout Advent. |
| Give a Christmas busker a bonus for playing a genuine carol. | Share the Christmas story with a child. |
| Smile at everyone you have to stand aside for in the supermarket or mall | Put a Nativity scene in a prominent place in your home or place of business |

# Christmas Parables

This devotional reading requires a leader and two readers

Leader: The most memorable teachings are conveyed by stories. Jesus never wrote a faith creed, a thesis, or a legal document defining his theology. Jesus told stories. We may not be able to recite a creed or quote long passages of Scripture but we all know the stories of the Prodigal Son and the Good Samaritan. We believe these principles are the essence of Christianity. Could it be, that inspired by the Jesus method, other teachers and writers spread the essence of Christianity by creating parables about Jesus?

Matthew: My name is Matthew. I am a Jew, but I no longer live in my homeland. I belong to a Jewish community in Antioch. I am passionate about my Jewish heritage; I fear it is in danger of being lost in this distant place. But I am even more passionate about the new insights of Christianity. My mission is to show my community how Christianity has grown out of Judaism. Jesus was a Jew who taught a new way of being and of understanding God. Jesus is greater than Moses, greater than King David, Jesus is Lord and Jesus is King.

Luke: My name is Luke. I trained as a medical doctor. I studied under Greek physicians. My desire was to help ill people gain health. Alas this is a difficult task, there is so much we do not know about how the body works and what aids healing. But I noticed that key to coping with illness is attitude of mind. Peace of mind and a positive disposition can bring health, even without curing the illness. I was so fortunate to encounter and learn from the apostle Paul. Now I want to put my Greek education to another purpose. I intend to write a book, a Good News account of Jesus.

Matthew: I have access to the Q documents and the writings of Mark. I will draw on those for the life and teaching of Jesus, but I must also connect to the old stories. First, I must set the scene in a way that enables my readership to understand just how amazing Jesus is.

Luke: I have access to the Q documents and the writings of Mark. I will draw on those for the life and teaching of Jesus. My work will be a pastoral Gospel that speaks of love and healing. First, I must set the scene in a way that enables my readership to understand just how amazing Jesus is.

Matthew: My telling of the story must proclaim the fulfilment of Scripture. Jesus is the promised Messiah, the Son of God. The telling of this story must appeal to Jewish men.

Luke: My telling of the story must be an inclusive account, a universal message of Good News that offers salvation to all. The telling of this story must also appeal to women.

Matthew: I've prayed about this and given it serious thought. I have wrestled with who is Jesus for me? For me he is my leader, Lord and King. His law supersedes the law of Moses. My Gospel will present Jesus as the new Moses. I will also draw on Joseph who saved his people in a foreign land. I will have my Joseph go to Egypt and return from that place. The Joseph of the Scriptures was carried from Egypt bound in mummifying cloths. The infant of my Joseph will be carried and bound in swaddling cloths.

Luke: I've prayed about this and given it serious thought. I have wrestled with who is Jesus for me? For me he is teacher, healer and a prophet who cares for all. He is a prophet even greater than Elijah. I will present Jesus as the new Elijah. When Jesus' work is done he will be taken up into Heaven. Elijah had encounters with women. My Gospel will include stories of women, and I will try to tell some stories from a women's perspective.

Matthew: The earthly father of Jesus is named Joseph; that is a good start. His father will be Jacob. The Joseph of the ancient scripture was a dreamer. Joseph will have dreams. He will talk with angels who will tell him how he should behave. However, our Jewish history begins with our Father Abraham. Our history and our religion are intertwined and inseparable. This must be a sacred story that uses sacred imagery. And I know just how to begin. I will use the holy numbers of three and seven. I will list the generations from Abraham to Jesus in a way that Jews can understand. Seven is a very holy number, twice seven will be seen as double holy. There will be 14 generations from Abraham to David, our greatest King; then 14 generations to the lowest point in our history, our deportation to Babylon; then a final 14 to the birth of Jesus our Messiah and Son of God.

Luke: All great men deserve an important birth. I will begin with birth stories – birth is a female thing; I will tell stories of women. The birth of Jesus will be a dramatic opening. I will build to a climax by first relating the story of his cousin who became John the Baptist, the one who proclaimed the coming of the Messiah. I will include a genealogy that stretches back from the father of Jesus to Adam, the father of the human race. This way everyone can claim a connection to the lineage of Jesus.

Matthew: My story will emphasise the Kingship of Jesus, his wisdom and greatness. I must include earthly Kings and wise men in my telling.

Luke: My story will show how Jesus relates to all society including the most marginalised. I must include lowly sheep herders in my telling.

Matthew: I will present Joseph as an honourable man, a righteous man who, like his namesake, behaves in an exemplary manner when confronted with a scandalous situation.

And I will show how Scriptures are fulfilled, "Look a young woman shall conceive and bear a son and they shall name him Emmanuel, which means God is with us.

Luke:  Mary, the girl God chose to nurture and birth the Messiah, must learn of this by talking with a messenger of God. Mary will speak with an angel. The angel will direct her to visit her kinswoman Elizabeth. It will be there that Mary understands the pregnancy. Mary is a girl, but Elizabeth is a wise and respected woman. She will give Mary guidance and point her to the Scriptures. The two of them will reflect on holy women who unexpectedly gave birth to important men. The holiest prophet of ancient times was Samuel. Mary shall learn and shape the words of his mother, Hannah, into a new song of praise.

Leader:  We cannot know the facts of the birth of Jesus. Ancient scribes did not view facts as we view facts. What we can be sure of is, people of that time were not interested in hearing of ordinary births. Like now, it is only after a person becomes famous that we want to know more about their background, and researchers go looking for origins.

Only Luke and Matthew offer birth accounts. Both tell wonderful stories, stories that present different messages for different people. They call us to ponder, who is Jesus for me?

Their nativity stories are the best loved stories of all time. They have inspired countless legends and nativity plays and they continue to inspire fresh tellings and new presentations.

All:  The messages given by Matthew and Luke are as wonder-filled now as they were then. We can ponder these things in our hearts knowing God is with us.

## The Twelve Days of Christmas

Exploring the religious symbolism of 'The Twelve Days of Christmas' we find that things might not be what they seem.

Throughout Advent reindeer, holly and fake snow decorate shopping malls all over New Zealand. If it isn't bad enough putting up with winter imagery in summer, mindless songs about Rudolf, kissing Santa, missing front teeth and partridges bombard our airwaves. These days we are hard-pressed to find any public Christmas trimmings remotely related to the birth of Jesus.

Christians often despair at the secularisation of Christmas. Instead of plunging into gloom take heart from historical Christian enterprise. From earliest Christian times the faithful have used pagan festivals to enhance the Christian message. The date for Christmas was carefully chosen to link with a Roman celebration that marked the shortest day had passed and light was coming. Easter takes its name from Eostre the goddess of spring.

One of the lesser known secular / religious combinations is the song The Twelve Days of Christmas. Why does such a nonsense song survive? It certainly has an appealing tune that has spawned many spoof lyrics. However, it is thought that the original nonsense had a purpose. The words are packed with religious imagery. This song originated in the 16th century when it was unsafe to practise any religion apart from the State religion. Dissenters devised fun songs in code to remind their young of religious lessons taught in secret.

This song celebrates the official Twelve Days of Christmas that extended from Christmas Day to Epiphany. Each phrase represents a religious concept in disguise.

> [Authorities vary regarding some numbers – one version may be Protestant, the other Catholic.]

| | | |
|---|---|---|
| 1. | **True Love** | Refers to God – the giver of all good gifts. The first day partridge speaks of Jesus as this bird will defend its young to the death. The pear tree represents the Cross, reminding us that Christmas and Easter are entwined. |
| 2. | **Turtle Doves** | Reminders of the temple sacrifice made by Mary and Joseph, or the Old and New Testaments. |
| 3. | **French hens** | Speak of birds owned only by the wealthy and equate to the three Kings or the Theological Virtues of Faith, Hope and Charity. |
| 4. | **Calling birds** | Indicate the four Gospel writers calling people to faith or the four Gospels. |
| 5. | **Gold rings** | Refers to the Pentateuch, the five 'books of Moses' considered as precious as gold. |
| 6. | **Geese a-laying** | Uses eggs / new life symbolism for the six days of creation. |
| 7. | **Swans a-swimming** | Refers to the seven Gifts of the Holy Spirit or the seven sacraments of the Roman Catholic Church. |
| 8. | **Maids a-milking** | Uses milk as a nurture symbol reminding us of the eight Beatitudes. |
| 9. | **Ladies dancing** | Portrays joyful expression evocative of the nine Fruits of the Spirit. |
| 10. | **Lords a-leaping** | Matches 'lord' with 'authority' representing the Ten Commandments. |
| 11. | **Pipers piping** | Associates music with the joyful message of the eleven faithful apostles. |
| 12. | **Drummers drumming** | Indicates a steady rhythm to live by and directs attention to the twelve beliefs enshrined in the Apostles Creed, the twelve sons of Jacob or the twelve Tribes of Israel. |

So be aware, secular nonsense can convey profound messages. The important thing is to find the message. Don't let the secularisation of Christmas tarnish your celebration. Remember joyful messages can be found by making creative connections. Be invigorated by the festive atmosphere and know this is one time of year we have every reason to equate celebration with the Jesus. At this time of year our young are conditioned to the word Christmas as representing something good. The Kiwi commercial Christmas gives us the opportunity to enhance the message.

## Christmas Journeys

A reading for two people.

Have a display of Christmas cards standing on the worship table or pinned to a notice board

Person 1:   Let's think about Christmas cards – another chore on the long list of Christmas preparation. Yes, but like the other Christmas chores eminently satisfying – so good to receive, knowing the sender has remembered you and wants to share a greeting and often news of their doings over the past year. Cards are an enduring tradition of goodwill complete with traditional illustrations. What pictures come to mind?

Person 2:   Mary and Joseph and a donkey, a distant town beneath a star, kings on camels, shepherds with sheep, worshippers in a stable and a baby.

Person 1:   Now consider secular cards – what images do you see? Traditional pictures include puddings and trees, families having fun, and most dominant of all Santa and his reindeer.

Person 2:   And what about modern New Zealand cards? Again, Santa is present sometimes wearing red shorts and lazing on a beach. Our cards often embrace holiday scenes caravans and tents, sailboats and canoes.

Person 1:   Can you find any common theme uniting these very different pictures?

| Person 2: | Mary and Joseph with a donkey, kings on camels, shepherds on foot, Santa on a magic sleigh, and holidaying families travelling to beaches and lakes. All these images include a journey. |
|---|---|
| Person 1: | Religious journeys are seen as pilgrimages, secular journeys as holidays. The Santa journey is the most epic journey myth of all stories, magically kept alive by global goodwill and adult intent on delighting children. Journeys are significant events. |
| Person 2: | At the heart of Christmas is a baby. Babies bring joy and proclaim the beginning of a life journey, babies carry hope and potential, and invite us to new beginnings. The Christmas Baby personifies the Light of the World. |
| Person 1: | Let's reflect on our personal journeys this year... |
| Person 2: | What is uppermost for you, good times or bad times?<br>Silently name the bad times... |
| Person 1: | Without any bad we would be unable to appreciate the good.<br>We are able to appreciate and rejoice in the good.<br>Silently name the good times... |
| Person 2: | We have safely arrived at the beginning of a new Christian year. In the past year our paths have wound through some dark times. Visualise unlit lamps in the shadows of your valleys. Now bring a memory, of a good time, or an act of kindness, to each lamp so it glows... |
| Person 1: | Look back on the row of lights and know the Light of the World was with you this year past and will be with you this year to come. |

Like shepherds and wise-men,
in our journeys we find you
in unexpected places.
We find you in our worries
and hear your words, fear not.
We find you in our wonders
and hear your words, behold
I bring you glad tidings.
We find you in quiet moments
and we know great joy.
As we put love in action
we participate in your hope
of peace and goodwill
for all humankind.
With the angelic chorus of
Glory to God singing in our hears
we will journey on knowing
you are with us, Christ Emmanuel. Amen.

## Spiritual Garden – Harvest Festival

This is a small group activity

Prepare a simple drawing of a symbolic church filled with people, and four sheets of paper (green A4) each with a picture (drawing or cut-out from magazine) of lettuce, turnip, squash, thyme and write the captions:

|  |  |
|---|---|
| (Lettuce) Let us be: | [kind, helpful, diligent, caring, willing…] |
| (Turnip) Turn up: | [prepared, on time, to give, to help…] |
| (Squash) Be sure to squash: | [gossip, discrimination, insensitivity…] |
| (Thyme) Make time to: | [pray, learn, smile, work, play, share…] |

**Divide into 4 groups**

- Give one picture to each group and a felt-pen.

- The groups compile lists to fit their caption.

- One person from each group reads their list then attaches it to whiteboard or notice-board under the caption 'Our church garden.'

- Complete mural by adding the symbolic people-filled church.

Leader:

> Look at the church garden we have made together. Water freely with patience and cultivate with love. As our plants grow may we...
>
> Grow in Grace and in the knowledge of our Lord and Saviour Jesus Christ. (2 Peter 3:18)
>
> Let us not grow weary in doing what is right, for we will reap at harvest time, if we do not give up. So then whenever we have an opportunity, let us work for the good of all. (Galatians 6:9–10)

Note: You can add a 5th vegetable – peas (peace) and the caption:

> (Peas) The peace of:   [love, understanding,
>                          consideration, harmony...]

Adding peas/peace can make this suitable for other Sundays not just Harvest Festival

### Garden Blessing

> Circle this place by day and by night,
> May cycling seasons bring delight.
> On our small garden may you smile
> and walk content with us awhile.
> Keep us aware of things that harm,
> and guide us to your healing balm. Amen.

# Palm Sunday – Christ Values

*Family Time:*

*What was special about Jesus of Nazareth?*
Sing: *A man there lived in Galilee*

Reflect on each verse. Do you agree with sentiments expressed?

*Considering Christian Values; Considering Christ Values*
- At small tables – write each value on a green frond (long, pointed piece of green paper).

- Christian Values – values you consider important for Christians.

- Christ Values – values Christ lived by.

- Make a palm leaf by sticking the fronds to a stem drawn on large sheets of paper.

- Discuss: Christian values on one left side of stem and Christ values on right side.

- Bring each sheet forward in turn and share how your group's choices were made.

*Concluding Reflection*
Back in the 18th century, John Wesley had a lot to say about Christian living. He lifted the spirits of the poor by telling them they were as important to God as the wealthy and they could be as good as any holy person. He devised a 'four-square' method for testing living a Christian life; beliefs and actions should be checked against four authorities. The system was called the *Wesleyan Quadrilateral*. The authorities were – *Scripture, Tradition, Reason* and *Experience*.

Two centuries later John A T Robinson, Bishop of Woolwich, wrote a little book called *Christian Morals Today*, by SCM Press. I bought a copy in 1965 at a bookstall in Exeter Cathedral for 2/6. It was only 47 pages, but it gave me much to think about.

Robinson said, "Moral theology starts from persons rather than principles, from experienced relationships rather than revealed commandments. But it does not disclaim authority."

I saw a connection with the *Wesleyan Quadrilateral*. Both Johnnies are revolutionary, but Robinson went further than Wesley, Robinson said, "There is no such thing as a Christian ethic. Times change, and Christians change with them. The only Christian command is to love; every other injunction is an application of it. Christian love is a deep concern for the other as a whole person."

And this is the thought I want to leave you with on this Palm Sunday. Christianity with all its morals, thou shalt nots and judgemental attitudes, is not what Jesus died for; nor did he die for 'our sins.' The 'sin concept' was an early theological attempt to reconcile ancient beliefs with a new religion. Jesus was a political rebel just as much as he was a deeply spiritual person. His vision of love in all its fullness, and teachings of respect for all, were threatening to the authorities. I believe the best way we can honour the death of Jesus is to live as resurrected people showing Christ's teachings in our lives, believing,

> The only Christian command is to love; every other injunction is an application of it. Christian love is a deep concern for the other as a whole person.

Pin mural palms to the easel board as groups share their findings.

## Dualities of Holy Week

This is a reading for several voices illustrated with pictures or symbols.

The pictures and symbols can be presented in a variety of ways. I presented this at a 'cafe service' and began by distributing coloured pictures and printed notes around the tables. Some of the pictures were hand drawn and others lifted from Sunday School resources. All were mounted on cardboard and turned into cut-outs. Volunteers sitting at the tables read the appropriate notes when I gave the heading, then two people came forward with the pictures and attached them with Blu Tack to the bamboo rod I was holding in a horizontal position.

| | |
|---|---|
| Leader: | Holy Week beings on Palm Sunday with... |
| Two Processions and Two Cries: | One Spring day, around the year 30, two processions entered Jerusalem at the beginning of the Week of Passover. From the east, a peasant preacher / teacher / healer from Nazareth rode a young donkey down the Mount of Olives cheered by peasant supporters. The core of the group had travelled, on foot, from the district of Galilee about 100 miles to the north. The enthusiastic supporters pulled fronds from palm trees, using them as hand-held flags. As Jesus rode by they shouted 'Hosanna.' |

On the opposite side of the city, Pontius Pilate, the Roman governor of Idumea, Judea and Samaria, entered Jerusalem at the head of a column of imperial cavalry and soldiers. He had left his villa by the sea, at Caesarea Maritima, some 60 miles to the west to be present with military might in case of trouble. It was the standard procedure of the time. The crowd that lined the route voiced the required 'Hail Caesar' as the Roman Governor passed by.

| | |
|---|---|
| Leader: | One procession proclaimed the Kingdom of God the other the power of the Empire. |
| Two sets of coins: | One set was merely two dull copper coins, so small they were known as mites. They belonged to a widow. While wealthy people gave impressive contributions to the temple treasury the widow made her small contribution – a contribution worth more than all the others because hers was all she had. |

The other set of coins were large, made from shiny silver. There were thirty of them, a king's ransom, blood money, paid to a man who betrayed his friend.

| | |
|---|---|
| Two Basins: | One basin was a common household vessel used for washing feet. This task was usually performed by a servant of the host. But not on this occasion, Jesus, the guest of honour, took a towel and the basin, and with humility washed the feet of all present. |
| | The other basin was an elegant bowl used for washing the hands of the powerful. Pontius Pilate ordered this bowl to make a memorable political statement. With an eye for the dramatic he publicly washed his own hands, demonstrating that he would have nothing more to do with this prisoner. |
| Two Whips: | One whip was small, made simply by plaiting cords. It was used to interrupt a wrong. In the name of religion, within the holy courts of the temple, money changers were robbing the poor by charging exorbitant fees. One man took action against this wrong. |
| | The other whip was large and cruel, made to shred flesh and used to flog an innocent man for political purposes. |
| Two Crowns: | Jesus was of King David's line. The Jewish expectation was for a messiah who would be a king-like liberator. Jesus was a king, but he had no use for a bejewelled Kingly crown. As he told his followers, my Kingdom is not of this world. In his final hours Jesus was ordered to stand before an earthly king one who delighted in all the trappings of office. King Herod was glad to meet Jesus as he knew him by reputation and hoped to be entertained with a performance of wondrous signs. |
| | The other crown was a mockery of kingship, a crown of thorns made to inflict pain. |
| Two Disciples: | Peter, the disciple we feel we know best, plunged through that week showing passion, bravado and ultimate fear of being recognised as 'one of those.' |

In contrast a lesser known disciple, not even one of the Twelve, risked telling the authorities he was 'one of them' by asking for the body of Jesus and placing it in a tomb he had prepared for himself. Joseph of Arimathea showed fearless compassion and devotion.

Two Gardens: The two significant gardens of Holy Week have been preserved down the centuries to our time, drawing pilgrims and tourists. The Garden of Gethsemane is fittingly bleak, consisting mostly of scruffy olive trees.

The Garden of the Tomb is vibrant with bright flowers and in the midst of the flowers there is an inscription "He is not here – he is risen." It is a place to ponder the mysteries of death and life.

Leader: 'He is not here – he is risen' has been interpreted in different ways from the beginning of Christianity. During Holy Week people of faith ponder these words and what they may mean for themselves.

This week is the most significant time in the Christian year. It is a time to reflect on passion and pathos, a time given to confronting evil and horror, a time to rejoice in goodness and hope, for ultimately life triumphs over death. It is a story of symbols and dualities, pairs and contrasts – a sacred story that enables us to live in the here and now as Easter People.

**Sing:** Bill Wallace's hymn: *We are an Easter People.*
Alleluia Aotearoa 146.

## Wisdom and proverbs

It is understood that the book of Proverbs was written as a book of instruction for young men and the final chapter that extols the virtues of a good wife employed a memorable teaching device. The verses of chapter 31:10–31 are cleverly arranged in acrostic form, each verse begins with a different letter of the Hebrew alphabet presented in alphabetic order.

So, for fun and edification, I have compiled, in English, an alphabet of Ancient Wisdom taken from the book of Proverbs.

Have on individual cards for a cafe congregation to read or present in a service with two people reading alternative verses.

### An Alphabet of Ancient Wisdom

Verse numbers are from the NRSV Bible translation

**A** soft answer turns away wrath,
   but a harsh word stirs up anger. — 15:1

**B**etter is a dinner of vegetables where love is
   than a fatted ox and hatred with it. — 15:17

**C**ommit your work to the LORD,
   and your plans will be established. — 16:3

**D**iscipline your children, and they will give you rest;
   they will give delight to your heart. — 29:17

**E**ven fools who keep silent
   are considered wise. — 17:28

**F**olly is a joy to one who has no sense,
   but a person of understanding walks aright. — 15:21

**G**o to the ant, you lazybones;
   consider her ways, and be wise. — 6:6

**H**appy are those who find wisdom,
   and those who get understanding. — 13:3

**I**t is better to live in a corner of the housetop
   than in a house shared with a contentious wife. — 21:9

**J**ustice…To do righteousness and justice
   is more acceptable to the LORD than sacrifice. — 21:3

**K**eep hold of instruction, do not let go;
   guard her, for she is your life. — 4:13

**L**et your father and mother be glad,
   let her who bore you rejoice. — 23:25

136

Make no friends with those given to anger,
and do not associate with hotheads, lest you learn
his ways and entangle yourself in a snare. — 22:24–25

Now my children, listen to me;
happy are those who keep my ways. — 8:32

Open your mouth, judge righteously,
maintain the rights of the poor and needy. — 31:9, (RSV)

Pride goes before destruction,
and a haughty spirit before a fall. — 16:18

Quarrel...whoever meddles in a quarrel of another
is like one who takes a passing dog by the ears. — 26:17

Riches do not profit in the day of wrath,
but righteousness delivers from death. — 11:4

Scoffers set a city aflame,
but the wise turn away wrath. — 29:8

Trust in the LORD with all your heart,
and do not rely on your own insight. — 3:5

Unjust...The unjust are an abomination to the righteous,
but the upright are an abomination to the wicked. — 29:27

Vinegar...Like vinegar to the teeth,
and smoke to the eyes, so are the lazy to their employers. — 10:26

Without counsel plans go wrong,
but with many advisers they succeed. — 15:22

'Xalt...Prize her highly, and she will exalt you;
she will honour you if you embrace her. — 4:8

Your friend, and your father's friend, do not forsake;
do not go to your brother's house in the day of your calamity.
Better is a neighbour who is near than a brother who is far away.
— 27:10 (RSV)

Zion...Let Israel be glad in its Maker;
let the children of Zion rejoice in their King! — Psalm 149:2

### A good life who can find?
An offspring of Proverbs 31:10–31

A good life who can find?
It is far more precious than jewels.
At the heart of a good life is trust;
trust in self, and trust in others.
Those who seek life do not harm;
they work with willing hands,
and listen with understanding.
They consider their options
and embrace the best path
with enthusiasm, hope, and joy.

They nurture with kindness,
perceive with wisdom,
and act with generosity.
They are not overwhelmed
when the bad times come;
for they are equipped
with determination,
and fortified by love.
Strength and dignity
is their outer clothing
and empathy undergirds all.

Those who seek a good life
balance work with play;
Show respect to all people,
And live as good stewards.
They are slow to judge,
quick to smile, and ready to praise.
Their blessings are counted as many,
and their wealth is beyond measure,
because they value relationships.

# The Full Jar — A children's talk / devotion

**Props**

A jar full of ping-pong balls, two smaller jars of pebbles and sand, takeaway container of tea or coffee.

## Explain

This jar represents your life. (Hold up large jar)

- These **balls** represent the important things: God, family, children, friends, and favourite passions. Things that if everything else was lost mean that your life would still be full.

- The **pebbles** represent other things that matter, like your health, job, house, and car. (Hold up pebble jar and add some pebbles to fill spaces round the balls)

- The **sand** represents everything else — the small stuff of life. (Add some sand)

If you put the sand into the jar first there is no room for the pebbles or balls.

The same goes for life. If you spend all your time and energy on the small stuff, you won't have room for the important things.

## Moral

Pay attention to the critical things.

Nurture relationships with God, partner, children, friends…

Work diligently; embrace a healthy lifestyle…

Set your priorities — the rest is just sand.

## The tea/coffee?

No matter how full your life may seem, there's always room for a cuppa with a friend. (Pour the drink into the jar.)

> Loving God we give thanks
> for the full lives we have enjoyed;
> We give thanks for those who helped us
> to recognise the big things in life
> and encouraged us to put them first in our way of living.

Our hope is that younger folk
may discern what is important
as they begin to fill their lives with the stuff of living.
May we never forget that life is a precious thing,
and every person is precious in your sight.

No one is too poor or too old to impact on others.
There are always choices to make and attitudes to hold;
Our hope is to stay positive and
act with wisdom and compassion;
Help us to stay mindful of Christ in all our dealings
and not forget that making time
to enjoy the company of friends
is part of the Jesus Way. Amen.

## Banana Heaven

(Similar to 'Survival by Cooperation,' but without active participation.)

Illustrate with a pair of stiff-arm dolls from the $3 shop and a banana.

This is a story about a toy-maker who had special powers. As well as designing dolls, she designed an afterlife for dolls to enjoy when they were no longer needed. All her dolls lived out their doll existence knowing that they had the chance of becoming real.

Discarded dolls disappeared to a testing place. Here it was decided whether or not the dolls had learnt enough to really live. At the testing place the dolls were transformed into living, breathing, eating, beings.

However, the transformation was not complete, one arm stayed doll-like stuck lifeless to a side. The other arm could move, up, down and sideways. The hand worked perfectly but the elbow wouldn't bend. In this almost transformed state the dolls were released in pairs to live in a testing garden. The garden was a pleasant place with shelter and water. The only food in the garden was a tree of ripe bananas. Dolls who lived happily for seven days were then completely transformed and able to join the dolls who were living happily ever after. Those who didn't manage to be happy together simply faded away.

Now, if you were those stiff-armed dolls how would you eat the bananas?

## Difficult Problems – 3 Sons and 17 Camels

Illustrate with camels drawn on cardboard and threaded on to a line. Begin with 17 camels.

Have two children hold the line and designate three others to be the sons standing behind the line.

> Once upon a time an old Arab died leaving his camel herd to his sons. The camel trader had three sons and he made provision for them in his will in the customary manner of the time. The eldest son, being the first-born would inherit half of his camels, the middle son would get one-third, and the youngest would get one-ninth of the herd.
>
> The sons wanted to obey their father's wishes, but they had a problem, at the time of his death their father had 17 camels. 17 is not a number that can be divided half, nor could it be divided by 3 or by 9. (Slide camels to illustrate)
>
> After several days thinking the situation became tense and the brothers decided they must seek help, so they made an appointment with the wise man of the tribe. The wise man listened to them patiently and asked them to return in the morning. When they returned the wise man said I have given you problem much thought. It pleases me that you want to honour your father's wishes, so I am going to gift you one of my camels.
>
> (Peg another camel to the line)
>
> Ask the children, "How many camels do you now own?" (18)
>
> Let's look at the will again?
>
> What is half of 18?
>
> (Children answer 9 and the eldest son puts his hands on the line marking his 9)
>
> The middle son is to get one-third, and one-third of 18 is?

141

(Middle son places his hands to mark his 6)

The youngest son is to get one-ninth – does anyone know what one 9th of 18 is? How many times does 9 go into 18? Yes, the answer is 2.

Youngest son takes two camels. What do you see? There is still one camel left over. The wise man said I will take this last camel as my fee for solving your problem.

This story proves that if you have a problem you can't solve, you need to ask for help. With the right help, when everyone wants a good solution, even really difficult problems can be solved.

If using this story in an 'Adult education' slot unpack it a bit more...

Each of the brothers left happy with the brilliant solution offered by the wise man – a solution that neither one of them had been able to come up with. Between the three of them, they left with the same total number of camels that they had come with, and yet, they left happy with the outcome, with no ill-will, with each of them feeling that it had been a fair solution to the problem.

So, what changed? In real terms nothing, but a peaceful solution had been arrived at that was acceptable to each of them. When they came, it was with the belief that a commonly acceptable solution could be found by consulting the wise old man. Believing in the possibility of an amicable solution is the first step for any negotiation to be successful, and the 18th camel became the common factor that neutralised the problem.

As is the case with many negotiations, believing that a common ground for a win-win situation can be found is critically important to finding amicable solutions. This helps to shape our attitude, and as is the case with anything else in life, a positive attitude can help to solve any kind of problem. However, a negative frame of mind distorts our vision and we are unable to see the possibility of a solution, which is most often the reason why negotiations break down. So next time we are stuck with any tricky negotiation, we first need to find that 18th camel.

## Mother's Day: Anna Jarvis (1864–1948)

Prepare several small baskets, some containing white and red flowers and some with pin-cushions and pins. Invite children to the front.

Show a picture containing lots of different people. It could be a montage made from magazine pictures.

Ask: What do all these people have in common? Some are short some are tall; they have different coloured hair; they come from different places; they do different things but every one of them was once a small baby and every new born baby has…? (A mother)

What day is it today? Why do we have Mother's Day? Did you do anything special for your Mum? Who is the most important mother in the world?

> Our Mother's Day comes from America. People in England have a different tradition and a different date. The story of our Mother's Day beings a long time ago It was the time of the American Civil War. All war is terrible but this one was very horrible because the Americans were fighting each other – brothers could be on different sides and possibly have to kill a member of their own family.

> In 1872 a lady called Julia Ward Howe wrote a protest hymn to help people understand how bad war is. But she didn't stop at hymn writing she was a thinking person with good ideas. She said, "No mother wants her sons killed. Let's get all the mothers saying, 'war is wrong.'" So, the first Mother's Days in America were about mothers saying no to war. When the war ended there was no need for a Mother's Day. But Mother's Day was not forgotten by the women of that district. A long time later a lady who had been a little girl during the war got another idea. Her idea was to have a day to remember the special things mothers do.

This lady was called Anna Jarvis. She was a teacher and very active in her church. Miss Jarvis convinced the leaders of her church that mothers deserve honouring. On the anniversary of her mother's death she brought baskets of flowers to church and asked each person to wear a flower – a white flower if their mother had died, and red flower if their mother was still alive.

The people thought it such a good idea they decided to do it next year and the year after. In fact, the church people thought it such a good idea they took the idea to their Synod, and then to Methodist Conference, and then to the Government. Miss Jarvis wrote lots of letters to important people including the President of the USA. Two years later in 1914, President Woodrow Wilson declared Mother's Day an official day to be celebrated on the second Sunday in May, the birthday of Anna Jarvis's mother.

And now our soloist is going to sing to us about mothers while our flower-girls hand round baskets of flowers. Our pin boys will follow up with pin-cushions. Please everyone – women, men, boys and girls – take a flower and wear it in memory of your own mother.

Note: Mothering Sunday as observed in the UK comes from a different origin and now is also called Mother's Day. It is celebrated on the fourth Sunday of Lent. Originally Mothering Sunday was a time of reunions when people returned to the church where they were baptised or attended services as children. It became customary for young people employed as servants in large houses to be given a holiday on Mothering Sunday to visit their mothers. Gifts of food or hand-me-down clothing were sometimes supplied by their employers. Being spring many picked wayside flowers for their mothers. These customs evolved to the modern tradition of giving mothers gifts or sending flowers.

Sundays are exempt from Lent fasts. The traditional cake for Mothering Sunday was Simnel (a light fruit cake with a layer of marzipan baked inside) covered with marzipan and decorated with 11 or 12 balls of marzipan, representing the 11 disciples and, sometimes, Jesus Christ. Legend says the cake was named after Lambert Simnel who worked in the kitchens of Henry VII of England around the year 1500.

# Father's Day

### *Ancient origins of Father's Day*
The ancient Roman festival of Parentalia, lasted from 13 to 22 February and was a festival of remembrance, commemorating departed parents. Ceremonies were held, Ovid says, "to appease the souls of your fathers." This annual observance became a family reunion. Members offered wine, milk, honey, oil and water at the flower-decorated graves, after which the living relatives enjoyed feasting together.

### *Modern origins*
New Zealand and Australia celebrate Father's Day on the first Sunday in September. Worldwide, Father's Day is celebrated in about 30 countries on a variety of dates. Dr Robert Webb of West Virginia is believed to have conducted the first Father's Day service on 15 June 1908 at Central Church, Fairmont. However, it was the colossal efforts of a woman known as Mrs John Bruce Dodd of Spokane, Washington, that led to a national observance.

When aged 27, Sonora Louise Smart Dodd conceived the idea while listening to a Mother's Day sermon. She had a small son and was the eldest child of a motherless family. Her father, William Jackson Smart, a Civil War veteran, was widowed by his wife dying in childbirth. William Smart raised the new-born and his other five children by himself on a rural farm in eastern Washington State.

> Mrs Dodd began her campaign by approaching the Spokane Ministerial Association and the YMCA. She hoped to have a local Father's Day celebrated on her father's birthday – the first Sunday in June. However, the Spokane Council could not get it passed on time but designated the third Sunday in June as the city's celebration for Father's Day. In keeping with the original Mother's Day tradition, Mrs Dodd suggested wearing a

red flower (a rose) to indicate a living father, and a white rose for a dead father.

In 1924, President Calvin Coolidge supported the idea of a national Father's Day after receiving a petition from Mrs Dodd and the custom spread throughout the States and the world. In 1936 a national Father's Day committee was formed. Headquartered in New York City, the committee annually selects a Father of the Year. Some of the fathers who have won this title are Douglas MacArthur, Dwight D Eisenhower, and Harry S Truman. However, it wasn't until 1966 that President Lyndon Johnson signed a proclamation officially declaring the third Sunday in June as the national Father's Day in the USA.

Why NZ decided on the 1st Sunday in Sept seems to be a mystery!

Ask children to draw around a 'gingerbread' father shape and fill it with descriptive words. Provide paper and pencils or biros.

If there are no children, share memories of your dad – your childhood; his qualities.

**Quotes to ponder on Father's Day:**
> When I was a boy of 14, my father was so ignorant I could hardly stand to have the old man around. But when I got to be 21, I was astonished at how much he had learned in seven years. (Guess who?)

*Mark Twain,*
*"Old Times on the Mississippi" Atlantic Monthly, 1874*

> Any fool can be a Father, but it takes a real man to be a Daddy!!

*Philip Whitmore Snr*

> The father who does not teach his son his duties is equally guilty with the son who neglects them.

*Confucius*

146

The most important thing a father can do for his children is to love their mother.

*Unknown*

My father gave me the greatest gift anyone could give another person, he believed in me.

*Jim Valvano*

He didn't tell me how to live; he lived and let me watch him do it.

*Clarence Budington Kelland*

I don't care how poor a man is; if he has family, he's rich.

*M\*A\*S\*H, Colonel Potter*

Don't make a baby if you can't be a father.

*National Urban League Slogan*

A man's desire for a son is usually nothing but the wish to duplicate himself in order that such a remarkable pattern may not be lost to the world.

*Helen Rowland (feminist!)*

By the time a man realises that maybe his father was right, he usually has a son who thinks he's wrong.

*Charles Wadworth*

Train up a child in the way which he should go
and when he is old he will not depart from it
(where from?)

*Proverbs 22:6*

## Meditation for Father's Day

Dear Dad,

I don't know how you did it, living to such a great age in perfect health. As for me my eyesight is starting to fail but I can still write if I hold the parchment close. I am a father myself of fine twin boys. Like you it didn't happen immediately. But I did what I could. I prayed, and God blessed us. The wife you bid your servant seek for me from distant kin, has proved to be all I could desire. When Rebekah stepped down from her camel it was love at first sight and has continued thus, but

147

being a father is not easy. This I now know and didn't know when you were around.

I will be frank Dad – there were times when I wished you were different. You were busy, an important man, head of a large household with many matters to occupy yourself with but for one who so desperately wanted children you gave us little of your time. Ishmael was 13 before you took any notice of him and then it was to cast him out. I felt it very wrong of you to banish your firstborn. He was my half-brother and we played together. I woke one morning to find my big brother had vanished. I was not able to even say goodbye. I missed my playmate and I missed his mother. Hagar was young and fun, a caring person, in retrospect a woman of great insight. I heard from the servants that you had sent them away because you wanted me to be your heir. At the time it made me feel special but later I realised it was not me for myself you wanted as your heir, it was me son of Sarah. Everyone knew Sarah was first wife and head wife. Surely you did not need to send Ishmael and Hagar into desert to fend for themselves. If it had to be you could have supplied men and donkeys to give safe passage.

But now my own sons are almost grown and I know from experience fatherhood is not easy. Children have their own personalities, being impartial can be difficult. I tried to be a better father than I felt you had been, but I confess a weakness in favouring my elder son. Esau is such a delight, an active lad, impetuous and daring. He has become a skilled hunter. I used to take both boys hunting. I saw that as part of the father's role, but the younger one had no heart for it. Jacob has brains alright, but he is a mother's boy.

Dad, I would have liked you to have taken me out hunting. That day when you sharpened your knife and told me I was going on an expedition with you was the best day of my life. My heart soared at the prospect of us spending father-son time together. I watched the preparations with such excitement I can recall each detail. You saddled your donkey and instructed two men to cut firewood. As we four trudged the trail together never had the sky been so blue or the landscape so beautiful. Two wonderful days of camping out then you told the men to wait with the donkey while just we two climbed the hill to make a sacred sacrifice. Remember how you loaded the wood onto my shoulders. I felt so proud that you considered me big enough for the task, but you kept glancing at back at me. It was a troubled look. I tried to reassure you that I could manage the climb. Then I saw tears in your eyes. I knew they were not tears of pride and joy. I couldn't understand. Was I failing this test of manhood? Had I let you down?

You didn't look at me again until I called out to you. It hit me all of a sudden that we had a knife and things for the fire but there was no sacrificial lamb. I was reassured by your reply and the way you waited for me to walk beside you. But when the altar was built I saw a new wild look in your eye. You seemed obsessed by some mission and you spoke to someone who wasn't there. I was frightened, very frightened. Your explanation made no sense. But I couldn't run away. This was the only thing you had ever asked of me. I didn't struggle as you bound me I wanted to appear brave. God came first with you and that is how it had always been.

Did you have any idea of my terror? You were my hero, and you let me down in the most devastating way possible! But, your God did not let you down. When I saw your attention taken by something that turned out to be a ram snared in a thicket, your God became my God. It took me a long time to trust you after that. But I grew to see you were a man of faith and you had capacity for human love. You had other wives, not a custom I have followed, but I know you truly loved my mother. When she died it was not just a tear in your eye, you wept floods. Then you sought a field with cave suitable for a fine burial. Even though you could have had it for nothing, you weighed out the market price of 400 shekels.

And it was there, dear Father, where Ishmael and I buried you. Yes Father, Ishmael and I eventually became close again. God had dealt kindly with him and his mother. Hagar was able to reach her Egyptian home in the court of the pharaoh and find a princess bride for your firstborn. Ishmael has become the father of 12 princes. I wanted to tell you this Father because I know deep down that you didn't want to send Hagar away. The way you did it was wrong, but you were torn by the frailties of human love. I understand frailties. I fear my frailty will come between me and my beloved wife. No one is perfect, but you taught me we can all trust in the perfect love of our God.

> Rest in peace Dad,
> Your loving son, Isaac.

Note: The age of Ishmael when banished by Abraham varies: in Genesis 21, Ishmael is an infant that his mother Hagar carried; in chapter 17, Ishmael is 13 years old

### *Father's Day activity*
Write things your dad taught you, or things you like (or liked) doing with your dad inside a kite shape or try creating a kite shaped faith poem from words.

### Kite Faith

Let us live life as
  Wide awake people
    Rise with celebration
      Soar with joy and hope
        Stay mindful that we of
          This faith community are
            Easter People committed
              To following the Jesus Way

                              for

                                now

                                  and

                                    for

                                      ever

                                        more

                                          yea

                                            and

                                              yay

# If You Were King

If you were a King or a Queen what would you want for your Kingdom?

I have four crowns here and I want four children to be my kings and queens. As you know kings and need to be wise and brave. I want the four brave volunteers to wear these (cardboard) crowns, sit on these thrones (chairs) and listen wisely while I tell a story.

Once upon a time there was a new king. He was a young king and he didn't want to be King. He much preferred being a prince but he had no choice. His father had been killed in battle and it was his turn to rule the Kingdom. It was not a large Kingdom, but it was a lovely place with mountains lakes and rivers and good farming land. It was bordered by four other kingdoms. As a prince he had been able to swim in the lakes and climb the mountains and ride his horse across the fields. His father told him he could only do this because the Kingdom was kept safe by soldiers who guarded the borders. The city where they lived was enclosed by a wall and if trouble threatened the heavy gates could be closed. At times the prince's father had to go away for a few days to calm trouble spots on the border and now he had been killed in one of these 'calming incidents.'

Ruling a kingdom is serious business. The new King didn't know where to begin, so he called for his advisors, the Lord High Chancellor and the Major General. "I need a plan," he said, "a strategy for ruling my Kingdom and keeping it safe, what do you suggest?"

"You must build more walls," said the Lord High Chancellor, "Every little village must have a wall to protect it."

"You must double the number of soldiers and allow more money for training and weapons," said the General. The King thanked his officials and said he would think about it.

After the officials had gone the King gave a great sigh because he knew there was not enough money in the royal coffers to do what either of his advisors wanted, and money was needed for so many other things like schools and hospitals and parks.

Now, the Jester had been in the room the whole time sitting quietly in a corner. This Jester had many talents including magic tricks, tumbling and juggling. Suddenly, the Jester sprang to his feet, did a triple summersault and bowed low. "Your majesty," he said, "allow me to lighten your load. If you will permit me I believe you have something in your pockets that you don't need," and from the three pockets in the King's gown he removed three balls and began juggling. As he juggled he talked, "These balls represent the worries of state – you have to juggle carefully to keep things going smoothly. Life is a balancing act," declared the Jester, standing on one leg and juggling the balls under his bent knee. "But being happy is the most important thing," he said catching all the balls as he did a back flip. The balls seemed to vanish into thin air and the Jester stood on his hands ginning at the King. The King couldn't help but smile.

Still on his hands the Jester continued talking, "When in doubt try a new perspective. Important people do not always give the best advice. Children often have good ideas why not ask some children what sort of a kingdom they want. They might even have some ideas as to how it could happen."

So, the King called for children, and invited volunteers for a royal task. He selected two girls and two boys. He gave them each a crown to wear and told them they were to think of themselves as Royal Rulers for the Day. "Your important task is to find ways to make everyone in our Kingdom safe and happy. Do you have any ideas how to make people happy?"

(Accept answers that come quickly, then say...)

Listening to people helps solve problems.

(Send the children to talk with someone in the congregation, after a brief time call them back)

Now, my 'Royal Rulers for the Day' you have given this matter consideration and listened to what others have said, what would make all the people feel safe and happy?

(Children share ideas prompted by adults with if required.)

The children of that faraway country decided the best thing to make everyone feel safe and happy would be to teach everyone to be kind to each other. If everyone was kind and friendly there would be no need for walls and weapons. Instead of fighting they could trade with their neighbours and there would be money for important things like parks and playgrounds. That is the sort of Kingdom that Jesus talked about and it is a Kingdom that we can be part of.

# The Tiny Town of Tontevoc

Written for Disability Sunday.

The tiny town of Tontevoc nestled in a sunny valley beside a sparkling river. It was surrounded by green fields backed by snow-capped mountains. Everyone lived in a warm house and no one went short of anything they needed. Instead of enjoying the good things they had the children of Tontevoc School were discontent. Each child thought some other child was more fortunate.

One child owned a pony, and another had a magnificent tree house. There was a girl who could run like the wind and a boy who could sing like angel. One girl was exceedingly pretty, and her brother was exceptional at sport. There were twins who didn't look alike and often argued. One family had four children at the school and they got to sleep in bunks. A girl who was very clever wore thick glasses. The boy who painted beautiful pictures lived with his grandmother. One child lived in a very fine house and had many toys. And, there was a boy who limped and had to use a crutch.

One day the wise-woman of Tontevoc visited the school holding a bunch of floating balloons. She looked carefully at each glum face then instructed the children to follow her to the field behind the school. "I can see you are you are dissatisfied with your lives. These balloons can help you be who you want to be." The balloons tugged on their strings as if they wanted to be free. "When you have each put your name on a balloon I will let go of the strings. While the balloons are floating you must think very carefully about what you want and who you would like to be. After a while the balloons will come down. Whichever balloon you choose to hold will become yours and you will become the person who owns that name. You will look like that child and live in that child's house and that child's family will not know you are really someone else."

As the balloons rose above the trees the children jiggled with excitement. Soon they would be pretty or clever or talented, live in a big house or own a pony or be able to run like the wind. But the balloons kept bobbing above the trees and the children kept thinking. Being a tiny town, everyone knew something about everyone else. The children thought about living in other families. Some families had teenagers or pre-schoolers to put up with. One father was known to get drunk. Some families didn't have two parents, and some had only one child. The rich girl had a nanny and hardly ever saw her parents. The twins got to thinking how they would miss each other terribly. The boy who walked with a crutch thought about his cute baby sister who made him laugh, and how his parents played with him and read to him. He thought of his grandparents who showed him interesting things and how they all hugged each other.

When the balloons finally drifted downwards the children ran, frantically searching for names, and grabbing at balloons. The boy with the crutch felt a great fear. All the others could run faster than him. When he reached the last hovering balloon, oh joy of joys, it had his name on it. He looked around. The other children were clutching balloons as if their lives depended on them – and each was thinking the same thought. The boy holding the last balloon smiled, the smile turned into a laugh and before long all the children were laughing.

A bunch of balloons would add interest if telling this story; having some filled with helium and letting them rise to the ceiling would be brilliant!

Note: When telling a story don't parrot the written script, make it live by using words that come naturally; where appropriate involve the audience (e.g. counting, booing or clapping); if not using props mime some actions (e.g. letting go of balloons and watching them float).

*Prayer*

God of goodness, gaps, and glitches
help us to see each other for what we are.

God of struggles, strengths, and strategies
help us to cope with what we have.

God of difficulties, disabilities, and delights
help us find joy in who we are.

God of individuality and invisibilities,
enable us to understand how life is harder
for some than it is for their peers;
Give us a readiness to ease difficulties,
remove barriers,
and create level playing fields

Bless us with the will to appreciate
the courage, creativity, and skills
required to live with impairment;
along with the discernment to realise
impairment is merely a fragment
of personhood.

Empower us all to live in fullness,
valuing what we have,
and knowing we are loved. Amen.

# The Prodigal Daughter

If telling rather than reading this story, illustrate it with a piggybank money box and two small dolls that can stand unaided and you can hold in each hand. Introduce them as sisters Anna (doll A) and Betsy (doll B). Hold them up and move them as appropriate. Or, choose two little girls willing to mime the action as the story is told.

Once upon a time there were two sisters who lived with their father and mother in an ordinary house in an ordinary street. Their mother did baking and grew flowers. Their father had a big vegetable garden. The elder sister, Anna, liked doing baking and she liked helping in the garden. The younger sister, Betsy, didn't like baking and the only thing she enjoyed doing in the garden was climbing the fruit trees. Both girls had jobs to do in the house and every week they were given pocket money. Half of what they were given was theirs to spend as they liked, the other half was put in a moneybox to save up for something special.

One Saturday afternoon when the rest of the family were working in the garden young Betsy was playing explorers in her bedroom. She had drawn a map and was planning an expedition. She had emptied her schoolbag and was packing it with things you would need for an adventure. (What would you need?) – a torch, a raincoat, some sunscreen, some chocolate, her water-bottle, a pocket knife and a compass.

The moneybox she was not supposed to touch was watching her. It was in the shape of a pig. The pig looked at her with his small piggy eyes and seemed to say, "Go on, I dare you to!" So, Betsy took that pig, turned him upside down, unscrewed the stopper in his tummy and shook out all the coins. Then she scooped them up and put them in the front pocket of her schoolbag. "Take that Moneypig! I am going on an adventure." Moneypig looked lonely sitting empty on the table. "You can come too," she said stuffing Moneypig into her schoolbag that was now a tramping pack. She put on the pack and her jungle sunhat.

"I'm going on an adventure," she sang as tramped down the street to the bus stop. Soon a bus came along. It had the words Railway Station above the front window. Betsy climbed on and said, "Railway Station please," and put down $2. At the station a few people were waiting in line at the ticket office. Betsy joined the queue, bought a ticket, and travelled by train right into the city. It was very exciting. She walked along the waterfront until she came to a park. No one was playing in the park but there was a tall slide in the shape of a lighthouse. Betsy played on it until the sun went behind a cloud. Even though it wasn't raining it felt cold. Betsy pulled on her raincoat and wondered what to do next. Actually, it wasn't great fun having an adventure all by herself, so she took out Moneypig. "What do you want to do Moneypig?" she asked. Moneypig looked at her with his black piggy eyes and Betsy remembered the chocolate. She pretended to share it with Moneypig. Then she gave Moneypig a slide, but he just tumbled over. It was getting windy. Betsy thought of the good dinner her mother would be cooking. Moneypig felt very light with no money in him. "I think you are hungry Moneypig," she said, "What do you think we should do?" Moneypig just looked at her with his little piggy eyes. (What do you think they should do?)

At the station they had a long wait for a train. For the first time that day Betsy thought about how her parents might be feeling. (How do you think her parents were feeling?) Betsy thought they might be angry that she had gone on an adventure. The more she thought the more she knew they would be very angry! Not only had she not told them where she was going, she had taken the money that she wasn't supposed to spend. All the way home on the train she practised what she would say to her parents. She was going to tell them she was very sorry and that she would stack the dishwasher by herself for a week and put all the clean dishes away. When she got off the train there was no bus waiting. It was a long walk to her house and it was starting to get dark. Suddenly she saw her father's car. He pulled up with a squeal of brakes. She started to say how sorry she was, but he wasn't listening, he was too busy giving her a big hug. Then Dad texted her mother and took her home. Mum and Grandma and Pop were all there. They had all been out looking for her. Betsy felt ashamed but they all hugged her and said how glad they were she was safe. Mum hadn't cooked any dinner because she had been too busy looking for Betsy.

Dad said, "Let's have a pizza party. We'll get chips and Pepsi as well, and you Betsy can choose any dessert you like from the menu." They didn't usually buy extras if they bought pizza.

Suddenly Anna ran out of the room and slammed the door. Her mother went after her and found her crying on her bed. "What is the matter dear?" she asked. (Why do you think Anna was crying?)

"It's not fair," sobbed Anna. "I'm always good and helpful and you've never had a pizza party for me."

Her mother hugged her close and said, "Anna, we love you very much and you make us so happy with your helpful ways. Both our daughters are special to us. Betsy was very naughty, and this made us very sad. We were worried about her. Bad behaviour always makes us feel sad, but nothing stops us from loving our children. We are having a party because we thought your sister was lost but now she is found."

# Meditation for Lent — A Light for All Seasons

Silently approaches spring
gliding on thawed angel wing
green shoots clasped in prayer
unfurl late in the antipodean year
our summer comes with angelic host
while northern folks have winter roast
we witness miracles of birth and flower
green the growth in our summer bower
Christ light comes
amid summer fun
a revelation here
a warm-fuzzy there
the lazy hazy days roll by
mindless of the clouding sky
autumn winds whinge apathy
stripping leaf from summer tree
spinning seed through savage air
the wrenching repeats every year
a Lenten chill lets good things die
the angered crowd cries crucify
blood lust appetites are whet
death they want death they get
then comes denial and despair
borne on stinging autumn air
we muffle our ears but see Christ bleed
hope is buried with the wind flung seed
but as is the kernel Christ springs eternal.

# A post Easter Reflection — The Emmaus Way

*(Luke, 24:13–35; John, 19:25)*

Between Easter and Pentecost, the Gospel readings focus on the appearances of the 'Risen Lord.' Like all Gospel stories, to the long-time-church-goer these stories are well-known, so well-known that they tend to flow over us and around us in a kind of comforting swirl. This is not a bad thing. Well-known stories become part of who we are. Good stories help make good people.

Church is meant to be a comfortable place where people can feel they are part of a family. But church is not meant to be too comfortable. It is not a place to kick off your shoes and blob out. In our worship tradition there is an emphasis on words The Word being prominent as a visual symbol and read passages an integral part of proceedings. Also important are words spoken in prayers and liturgy, the singing of our faith in poetry set to music and the words listened to.

The many words that comprise a service range through worship and wisdom to comfort and confrontation. Sermons / reflections have a variety of purposes, lulling people to sleep is not one of them! That said, providing space for mind wanderings and private soul searching, may be of more benefit than listening to the preacher.

Today, I am inviting you to step back from the well-known resurrection stories and ask yourself a question: Would it matter if those stories were not meant to be taken literally?

Would it make any difference to how you live your life?

Obviously, your answers will vary, and just as obviously there is no way any one of us can prove or disprove reported events of 2,000 ago. The message I want to present is: it is OK to wonder. When it comes to faith we each have to sort out for ourselves what makes sense to us. Holding differing opinions is natural and right. We are each shaped by our experiences and our own convictions. The only wrong position to hold on any issue is a position that causes harm. If your beliefs cause hurt to others, or yourself, you need to rethink your position. You may need help to do this well.

The stories of a culture carry the hopes and fears of the culture. For Christians the Holy Bible is the book of our religious heritage. We do the Bible a disservice if we read it with the eyes of modern newspaper readers. Bible stories were not recorded as events happened. Ancient peoples did not have devices for recording pictures and sound, not even pocket notebooks and biros. History was not viewed as verifiable fact. History was story with meaning. Much of the OT began as oral tradition that was reflected on and reshaped over many years of re-telling. The Gospels were written 30-60 years after the death of Jesus. Even with the possibility of some eyewitness accounts be mindful that the reports were filtered over many years and reviewed in the light of the epistles and early church teachings.

The Emmaus Road incident is a situation we can identify with. We readily understand the feelings of horror and defeatism the crucifixion must have brought to the followers of The Way. This man Jesus, a landless peasant from an obscure northern province, had moved from carpenter to itinerant preacher bringing a message so astounding that even the pagan authorities took notice. His message was that God, the great creator of the universe, the one whose name was too sacred to even speak, actually loved all people – the poor, the ill, the infirm, the marginalised, even women. The mighty creator God did not require money or sacrifice, not even obedience! All God required was that you love others as God loves you.

The concept is so 'old hat' to us we can't possibly comprehend the gob-smacking impact it must have had on the first listeners. The young man Jesus was a radical. His teaching was a revelation, an epiphany of joy.

At the time Palestine was an oppressed country under Roman occupation, but its people had suffered under various oppressors for generations. Not only were successive governments oppressive, so was its religion. Now, don't get me wrong here, Judaism was probably the best religion around. At the same time the Jews were firming up on what God was like and what was required of them, the Greeks, Romans and Nordic people were evolving stories of Zeus, Jupiter and Woden – hedonistic gods who trifled with humans for sport.

The Jews had a concept of a just and righteous God, a God of Covenant who required moral behaviour in all aspects of life, a far cry from the gods of Jewish contemporaries. But they became carried away by visions of holiness and developed an oppressive regime of rules and rituals, regulations and religiosity that deemed the masses as unacceptable in the sight of God.

Enter Jesus, who taught that God was like a forgiving parent. The Jews knew the love of God was steadfast, the psalms assured them of this, but the psalms also assured them God was a vengeful God ready to inflict punishment at any turn. They believed they were God's chosen people and that this came with conditions. The priests interpreted the condition as making lots of punitive laws. The role of God was to punish the sinful.

Jewish law pushed the maimed, the ill, the mentally disturbed and sinners to the edges of society. But Jesus ate with known sinners and welcomed the marginalised among his friends. Jesus saw women as individuals not as the property of males. Jesus exampled unconditional love and taught it was not the fault of individuals that ill had befallen them. God loved and cherished each person. Jesus put doing good above obeying the law. Wowee! This is ground breaking theology – a theology that brought tremendous hope to the people of his time, and to people of all generations, ever since.

So back on the road to Emmaus… an ordinary couple returning home after celebrating the Passover in Jerusalem. What do we know about them? Not much. Only one is named and his name is Cleopas. The other has no name and was presumed to be male. Why? Is it not more usual for a man and woman to be living together, as these two obviously were! The name Cleopas is only one letter different to Clopas. There are many examples in the Bible of a person's name being spelt in different ways. Among the women at the cross was one identified as Mary wife of Clopas.

[Preacher drapes a headscarf over own head or has a woman, with headscarf, read from lectern]

### Wife of Cleopas
My name is Mary, wife of Cleopas, and I want to give my testimony. Cleopas and I had walked to Jerusalem many times. Our village of Emmaus is only seven miles from the city. We usually manage to be there for Passover. For us Passover is an important ritual as well as a time of celebration and remembering who we are and from whence we came. Usually the walk home is made with

light steps. But this year our hearts had never been so heavy. We had witnessed dreadful things, terrible things. We saw Jesus the Rabbi whipped and humiliated. How could they be so cruel to anyone, let alone this good man? We knew Jesus as the healer who preached a way of love and respect for all. He went about doing good. Goodness is a powerful thing, too powerful for the Romans – they felt threatened. To them he was a political rebel. The lies and wild accusations were incredible, but Jesus remained dignified throughout. It was too much for our men. They couldn't bear it but we women stayed to the very end. Even on that hideous cross his concern was for his mother.

Well, as I said, we were journeying home. I was telling Cleopas the last words we women heard Jesus speak and explaining how the end came, when we were joined on the road by a stranger. He asked us what we were discussing. His question was so surprising we stopped still in amazement. Cleopas said, "Are you the only stranger in Jerusalem who does not know the things that have taken place there in these days?" He wanted to know what things.

So, we told him how Jesus of Nazareth was a prophet who had been crucified, that hideous form of execution favoured by the Romans. Although his body had been put in a decent tomb it had vanished and we were sad, sad, sad. This wonderful man, whom we had thought of as Lord, was dead and now his teachings would die. His teaching had given us such hope. In essence they were simple beliefs based more on hospitality and caring than on following rules.

But we soon discovered our companion was no ordinary man. He knew the Hebrew Scriptures and he expounded them to us as we walked along. He also knew of the way of Jesus. The way he talked brought warmth to our heavy hearts. When we arrived at our village it was nearing evening. We urged the stranger to come and have a meal with us.

It didn't take me long to rustle up a simple meal. I didn't even feel tired. When we sat at table the stranger took the bread, blessed it, broke it and gave it to us. At that moment we saw Jesus in the man. The revelation was so powerful we were quite stunned. By the time we had recovered the Jesus man had gone.

It was a startling revelation for both of us. We realised the death of Jesus was not the end of the Jesus Way – if the ritual of the fellowship meal could continue, why not the teachings? We were so excited that as soon as we had eaten we went straight back to Jerusalem. We found the eleven disciples together and they were celebrating, saying, "The Lord has risen indeed."

*[1,675 words]*

Let us read together the prayer printed on your service sheet...

Be known to us in breaking bread
be known to us in hospitality
be known to us in strangers
be known to us in friends
May the way to Emmaus
also be our way
travelling with
shared story
open minds
warm hearts
shared food
and celebration
Living God, may we never neglect to invite you in, Amen.

## The Thirteen Precepts

Moses ben Maimon, or Maimonides, as he known was an important Jewish scholar. He was born in Spain in 1138 and died in Egypt in 1204. His father was a Jewish philosopher. Maimonides became one of the most influential Torah scholars of the Middle Ages. One of his many enduring writings was a summary of Jewish belief called the *Thirteen Precepts* or 'principles of faith' that are still a mainstay of traditional Jewish belief. Maimonides' first three precepts are:

1. God is the creator and guide of everything that has been created.

2. God is One, and there is no unity like His.

3. God has no body and He is free from all the properties of matter.

Not statements that are likely to enthuse us, but the concept is interesting. We have moved away from creating lists of things to believe preferring to realise our faith by what we do. So, what are the hall marks of our faith?

Today we are going come up with our list of 13 principles of Faith. Each table has a sheet of paper and a pen. Turn the paper over and decide on the 13 principles or qualities you see as important definitions of a Christian person. I offer three suggestions and ask your group to supply a further 10.

Prepare sheets headed:

### Thirteen Principles of Christianity

We believe a Christian should:

1. Follow the loving example of Jesus

2. Show compassion at all times

3. Look for good and God in everyone

# God in Nature

[Same process as *Thirteen Principles of Christianity* above with a different topic)

Today we are thinking about God in nature and ways that we may have a spiritual experience though nature: I offer three suggestions and ask your group to supply a further 10. Prepare sheets headed:

## Thirteen Spiritual Interactions with Nature

We believe that it is a holy act to:

1. Walk barefoot in the grass.

2. Encounter a rainbow.

3. Watch a sunrise.

[Suggestions for you to have in reserve if hints are needed]

4. Bask in the rays of the sun.

5. Stand in an open space on a clear starry night.

6. Climb to the top of a hill.

7. Scan the horizon over the sea.

8. Swim in ocean, lake or stream feeling supported by water.

9. Take a gulp of country air at night, after rainfall.

10. Scrunch through Autumn leaves.

11. Feel sand run through fingers and toes.

12. Tend a garden.

13. Encourage our young to experience God by: building sandcastles, jumping in piles of leaves, splashing in puddles, flying kites, rolling on grassy slopes, paddling in the sea, hugging trees, smelling flowers, picking fruit and wondering at creation.

## Seeds and Flowers

Sing: *I come to the garden alone...* (No hymn books needed if you provide a soloist and have the congregation join in the chorus)

It is easy to feel close to God in a garden. This is not surprising. In the very beginning of time God planted a garden. Our oldest tales tell of human-kind experiencing God in a garden. God walked and talked with the first humans in the context of a garden. That garden represented perfection.

Consider a garden that you know and love ... and words that describe gardens ... beauty, serenity, peace, fragrance, creativity, variety, growth, abundance.

A garden is a place to relax and enjoy, but it also a place of work. The best gardens are formed by God and humankind working together. Humans bring ideas and labour, but without God's blessing of life and growth, there is no yield.

> Pass round a bowl of mixed seeds – poppies to pumpkin, nuts to nasturtium. Ask everyone to take a seed and ponder its potential while listening to music (e.g. recording of *Our Life Has Its Seasons* Alleluia Aotearoa 113 – track 2 on the Alleluia Aotearoa CD)

The seed you hold came from a container of mixed and unlabelled seeds. Some of you may know what kind of seed you hold for some are readily identified but there are millions of others that no one here could identify. But all of us know whatever the seed it has the potential to sprout and grow.

Today we are celebrating (Spring Flower Sunday, Harvest Festival, Season of Creation...) or, we are at the beginning of (a year, spring, summer...) We do not know what this season / year holds for us. But we do know that all seasons / years have the potential for growth. The seeds of many flowers are so insignificant we can barely see them. Individual seeds can be too small to pick up. Yet within the insignificant fragment is carried the potential for colour, fragrance and joy. Flowers bring beauty to the world. Place the seed you selected in your pocket or purse. Now we are going to look at seeds that have transformed into flowers.

167

Pass round a basket of mixed flowers while more music is played.

You hold in your hand a flower. See what an amazing thing a flower is: consider its colours ... each flower is multi-coloured or delicately painted in hue variations. Note its shape, the number of petals and its centre with stamens, pistil and pollen. Note its texture – the unique fabric of a petal that has not been spun or woven, needled or knitted. Consider its delicacy as you brush it against your cheek. Reflect how each flower variety comes with its own unique leaves, roots and plant form. Test your flower for perfume – not all flowers are blessed with fragrance, but each has a beauty of its own.

As you gaze on the flower you hold remember it sprang from a tiny seed. We do not know what will happen in our lives this year / season, but we know we have the potential for growing closer to you ... May we too bring beauty to the world. Let us pray.

> We are called to live fully,
> We are called to love extravagantly,
> We are called to be the very best people we can be,
> We are called to grow. We can be agents of joy.
> We commit ourselves to follow
> the loving example of Jesus.

## Invigorating Bible Stories

[Particularly suitable for Bible Month, July]

As fewer parents are encouraging their young to read the Bible, church going grandparents, great-grandparents and great-aunts/ uncles are the prime people to 'pass it on.'

We 'grands' and 'greats' grew up in an era when the importance of the Bible was an accepted given – students at state schools heard the Bible read by a prefect at the weekly assembly. Persons speaking in court swore on the Bible as the most sacred token of truth in our society, fearing the wrath of God should they not tell the truth. Bible stories were well-known. This knowledge helped bind us in a community of shared values.

Life is very different today. There are no unchallenged 'givens.' Our 1960s Global Village concept of the world as a unit where people care about each other in practical ways, has been overwhelmed by the reality of a Global City of mixed races, cultures and religions, where neighbours are not known and 'self first' prevails. With the IT explosion our children are exposed to images of everything – some wonderful, some dangerous, some helpful, some harmful, but all educational – be it for good or bad.

The bits of the Bible that make an impact are not the verses children were once expected to commit to memory. The bits that stick are the stories. People of all religions, and none, know of Eve's encounter with the snake, Noah's Ark and the Christmas story. Christians have failed to realise the worth of story. We have been too hung up on 'is it true?'

The Bible was compiled when common knowledge saw the world as a three-tiered universe with Heaven and Hell enclosing a flat earth between two basins. It was the era of Sky Gods, when men, and I use the word deliberately, looked up in awe to the Heavens where they believed the good gods lived. Speaking very generally women have been more drawn to the concept of nurturing earth-mother goddesses who inspire looking within the self. Sky gods cause humans to look up with awe; sky gods affirm the valiant; sky gods are kings and warriors. Reaching deep into one's spiritual self is right and good, but it is only one half of the spiritual coin. Might and majesty are also good.

Story is the most powerful of educators. All cultures explore what it is to be human by creating their own cultural stories. The people of that tribe or nation know those stories and through that shared knowledge they know and shape who they are. Stories are part of their language and give shortcuts to verbal expression.

The power of story is not in facts, the power of story is its message and how we apply the message. We have always known that parables didn't happen as historic fact but that doesn't make The Good Samaritan of any less value. The same applies to other 39 parables of Jesus. They are stories with a spiritual purpose. What if we looked at the whole of the Bible in this way?

A danger for life-long attending church goers is that Bible stories become so familiar they lose their impact. Revitalising well-known Biblical stories is a way of discovering fresh insights.

We have always done this for children. But why keep the good stuff for them! There are adult ways to revitalise the old stories. One way is fleshing out the stories by taking the facts supplied in the bible and applying some creative imagination, while remaining true to the original text, thus feeling into the character as a multi-layered person, such as would appear in a novel.

Jesuit priest Patrick Arnold, in his book *Wildmen, Warriors and Kings* (1995) acknowledged the fine work done by feminist theologians that can enhance the scriptures for all and urged us to reclaim God in a masculine way that can also enhance the scriptures for everyone.

Arnold's method of making Bible characters live, is to not think of them as complex individuals, but to engage with them as we appreciate characters in folk story – persons we readily recognise as villain or hero, or in other words as archetypes. This adds a powerful dimension of defined qualities that we can relate to and learn from. Thinking of Biblical characters as archetypes does not lessen their worth or godliness. It is a way of maximising the power of the story.

### Background Input to 'Archetypes'
The term "archetype" has its origins in ancient Greek. The root words are *archein*, which means "original or old;" and *typos*, which means "pattern, model or type." An archetype is a primal pattern of thought—inborn, instinctive, and imprinted on every human's subconscious mind.

The Swiss psychologist, Carl Jung used the concept of archetype in his theory of the human psyche, proposing that universal, mythic characters, archetypes, reside within the collective unconscious of people the world over. Archetypes represent fundamental human motifs of our experience as we evolved and encompass love, religion, death, birth, life, struggle, survival etc. These experiences exist in the subconscious of every individual and are recreated in literary works or in other forms of art in all cultures.

By looking at Bible characters as archetypes we get an understanding of roles and models. Kings should be mighty leaders who respect God (and we don't need get hung up over the way David treated his many wives). Kings should have wealth and wisdom and respect God (and we aren't compromised by the fact that Solomon's heavy taxes brought the downfall of the nation – not that many church goers realise this). The passages we hear in church are carefully selected and sanitised.

Elijah's archetype is the wild-man, who emerged from nowhere, a confrontational man, staunch in the face of danger yet a man who knows fear. In fear he is receptive to the spiritual – he hears the voice of God not in earthquake, wind or fire, but in a still small voice of calm. Elijah protects widows and children, but his greatness lies in his faith. For the one true God he is prepared to stand up and be counted. In this he is a magnificent, manly role model (and we don't need be bothered by him killing 450 of Jezebel's prophets). To add insult to injury Baal was, among other things, the great god of weather. After his priests were slain there was the gratifying sound of 'rushing rain.' What a victory! There was nothing half-hearted about Elijah's faith. The moral is – put your trust in God.

Elisha has different qualities. Elisha serves a prophet apprenticeship and although he takes up the mantle of his master he avoids confrontation with royalty, though he does take an extreme defensive position towards small boys who call him baldy (and in the context of folk story we don't need to be distressed by his action)! Elisha is a mystic, a shaman healer who fixes things and acknowledges God as the true healer.

Assigning Bible characters to archetypes is a liberating exercise … Typically we think of Moses as leader and law giver, but he can also be seen as a magician and just as interesting as Gandalf or Dumbledore; Jacob can be seen as trickster; Jonah the fool who tries to flee from God etc.

Children and young people are into this sort of thing through action movies and computer games. By matching Bible character to archetypes, you can explore what the Bible means to you, in a fun way that you may be able to share with young people, and thus pass it on.

### Participation time

The following activities could be done as a simple oral exercise, or with a prepared whiteboard and scribe, or as a written exercise in pairs or small group working from prepared sheets.

### Define some typical archetypes

Characteristics of folk-story characters – time permitting.
name examples from literature or history.

| Archetypes | *[Don't print the words in italics]* |
|---|---|
| Patriarch | *Family head, position unchallenged, decision maker.* |
| Matriarch | *Head of domestic household, notices details, nurturing.* |
| Trickster | *Ambitious, uses trickery for self-advancement.* |
| Leader | *Grasps situation, makes bold decisions, gets respect from followers.* |
| Magician | *Insightful, has special powers, uses magic to achieve results.* |
| Priest | *Mediates between the people and the Divine, performs rituals.* |
| Hero | *Brave, a leader prepared to do more than could be expected.* |
| Fool | *Appears incompetent, brings light relief to surrounding drama.* |
| Everyman / Everywoman | *Ordinary person on life's journey.* |
| Seducer | *Someone who tempts others to sin.* |
| Poet | *Dreamer of visions. May use words or music to reveal insights.* |
| King | *Ruler, his word is law, has trappings of wealth and power.* |
| Queen | *Wealthy consort with a limited measure of power.* |
| Judge | *Wise, skilled in arbitration, makes decisive moral decisions.* |
| Hermit | *Thinker who lives alone but will give advice to seekers.* |
| Prophet | *Spiritual person to whom truth is revealed, that he must proclaim.* |
| Shaman / Healer | *Gifts of healing and knowing, may be knowledgeable with plant remedies.* |

| | |
|---|---|
| **Maiden** | *Innocent, trusting, pure, of good intent.* |
| **Youth** | *Has enthusiasm and potential, willing to learn, risk taking.* |
| **Child** | *Innocent and trusting.* |
| **Wise Woman / Witch** | *Woman with accumulated wisdom and special powers.* |
| **Villain** | *Self-serving person who gets pleasure from doing evil.* |
| **Herald** | *Goes before and announces or proclaims of a greater person.* |
| **Traitor** | *Lets down those who had his trust.* |
| **Saviour** | *Has answers; is able to save situation; show a better way of being.* |

## *Fit all these Biblical characters into likely archetypes*
Guess any you don't know

> Note: An archetype is not static throughout life's journey – some characters fit in more than one archetype (cross out characters as you go – 1, 2, or 3 cross outs per person)

> Aaron, Abraham, Adam, David, Daniel, Delilah, Eli, Elijah, Elisha, Esther, Eve, Herod, Huldah, Isaac, Isaiah, Jacob, Jonah, Joseph, Joshua, Jacob, Jeremiah, Jesus, Jezebel, Joseph, Joshua, John the Baptist, Judas, Martha, Mary Magdalene, Mary of Nazareth, Miriam, Medium of Endor, Moses, Noah, Naomi, Peter, Pharaoh, Rachel, Rebecca, Ruth, Samson, Samuel, Sarah, Solomon, Timothy, Zachariah.

| **Bible Characters** | *[Don't print the words in italics]* |
|---|---|
| **Patriarch** | *Abraham, Isaac, Jacob* |
| **Matriarch** | *Sarah, Naomi* |
| **Trickster** | *Jacob, Samson* |
| **Leader** | *Joseph, Moses, Joshua* |
| **Magician** | *Moses, Aaron* |
| **Priest** | *Aaron, Eli* |
| **Priestess/Prophetess** | *Miriam, Huldah* |

| | |
|---|---|
| **Hero** | *Joshua, Noah* |
| **Fool** | *Samson, Jonah* |
| **Seducer** | *Eve, Delilah, Mary Magdalene* |
| **Poet** | *David, Miriam* |
| **King** | *Pharaoh, David, Solomon* |
| **Queen** | *Jezebel, Athalia, Esther* |
| **Judge** | *Deborah, Solomon* |
| **Hermit** | *Elijah, Jeremiah* |
| **Prophet** | *Samuel, Elijah, Elisha, Isaiah, Jeremiah* |
| **Shaman/Healer** | *Elisha* |
| **Maiden** | *Rebecca, Rachel, Ruth, Mary of Nazareth* |
| **Child (innocent & trusting)** | *Samuel, Miriam* |
| **Youth (idealistic)** | *David, Daniel, Timothy* |
| **Everyman/Everywoman** | *Adam, Eve, Peter, Leah* |
| **Wise Woman / Witch** | *Medium/Witch of Endor, Anna, Martha* |
| **Herald** | *John the Baptist* |
| **Preacher** | *Peter, Paul, Barnabas* |
| **Villain** | *Pharaoh, Jezebel, Herod* |
| **Traitor** | *Judas* |
| **Saviour** | *Jesus* |

Finish participation time with a plenary session where the groups call out their answers.

Give brief details on any unknown characters.

# 19 — Sample Prayers

There are many fine books of prayers. All worship leaders need to own some. (See the suggested list in Chapter 21 — Additional Worship Resources).

Prayers for church are different from prayers used in private devotions. A formal church service is not the place to use extemporary, off-the-cuff prayers. Most people who readily pray in public in this manner are unaware how often they repeat themselves or overuse a particular word or phrase – the word 'just' being a prime example as in, 'we just want to...'

Begin by using prayers composed by others. Acknowledge the source in italics. When sufficiently confident write some liturgical prayers of your own.

Unless otherwise identified all prayers in this book have been written by me, the reason being issues of permission and copyright. You are welcome to use or adapt my prayers without seeking permission but if you are printing them please acknowledge this book as the source. I have grouped the prayers in the order of the traditional liturgy.

- Calls to Worship

- Prayers of Approach

- Before the Reflection / Sermon

- Offertory / Offering

- Pastoral Prayers

- Benediction/Commission

- Prayers for Special Sundays

- Famous prayers

- Other Prayers

*Prayer Folder*

I recommend you compile you own collection of prayers that appeal to you. Cut them out of other people's service sheets or print them from your computer. I keep my cut-outs and favourites in an A5 pocket folder that I've divided into sections as listed above. I also keep a comprehensive computer file of prayers.

## Calls to Worship

Kia ora tātou!
**Kia ora!**

God be with you,
**And also with you.**

We are gathered as parishioners of ___ Church,
**We come as people blessed by location and means,**
**We come as people open to learning and sharing.**

Come citizens of Aotearoa, come and worship.

• • •

God is with us.
**Our faith is in you O God,**

Help us to know your ways,
**Lead us, teach us, inspire us;**

You are the One who makes us whole,
**And so we come to worship you.**

• • •

The Peace of God be with you
**And also with you.**

Travellers on the journey,
Rest awhile and reflect.
We release our burdens,
**And gather with expectation.**

Beware! God resides in this space.
Worship can change us.
**We are aware – we come to meet with God.**

God is good.
**Creation is good,**

The work of God is good,
**We are the work of God.**

We look for good in all things,
**We look for God in all people,**

We are ready to worship.

• • •

Life is a process of growth and development,
**We come for nurture to keep us growing,**

May our worship bring life and greening;
**Ever ready for new possibilities,**
**We are ready to worship God!**

• • •

Good morning God,
**We are one of your faith families;**

Bless us God,
**Help us open ourselves to you;**

Bless us God,
**May we hear your words and**
**understand your hopes for us;**

Bless us God,
**Bless us all, everyone!**

• • •

Kia ora tātou! Kia ora!
Wherever we are, wherever we go,
**the wonders of God surround us.**

Here we rejoice in the immediacy of hills,
sparkling waters, and pleasant gardens.
**These wonders tell of God's glory.**

The simplicity of a smile, the warmth of touch
and the hearing of a story;
**These too, tell of God's glory**
**We come with thanks and praise.**

• • •

May God be with you,
**And also with you.**

We come from differing places and differing spaces;
**We come because you have called us.**

We come knowing you are in all spaces and in all places;
**We come confident that you care for each of us.**

We come knowing you can be seen in all our faces;
**We come to worship the God of grace.**

*For Waitangi Sunday*
Kia ora tātou!
**Kia ora!**

God be with you,
**And also with you.**

Come parishioners of _____ Church,
**We come as people of a Covenant.**

Come citizens of Aotearoa, come and worship.
**We come as people of The Treaty.**

Come as one people.
**United, we come to worship.**

*Trinity Sunday*
May the beauty of God silence us,
**May the justice of Jesus give us voice,**

May the breath of the Holy Spirit enable us;
**May the fear of God expose us to truth,**

May the integrity of Jesus hold us to truth,
**May the power of the Holy Spirit be with us.**

178

Calls to Worship can be taken from Psalms:

> Open to us the gates of righteousness,
> **That we may enter through them**
> **and give thanks to the Lord.**

> The stone that the builders rejected
> has become the chief cornerstone.
> **This is the Lord's doing;**
> **It is marvellous in our eyes.**

> This is the day the Lord has made;
> **Let us rejoice and be glad in it.**
>
> *From Psalm 118*

Calls to Worship can be taken from hymns:

(Acknowledge authorship. Essential if written within the last 50 years.)

> Worship the Lord in the beauty of holiness,
> Bow down before God, God's glory proclaim;
> With gold of obedience and incense of lowliness
> Come now before God and honour God's name.
>
> *Adapted*

> Morning has broken like the first morning:
> Blackbird has spoken like the first bird.
> **Praise for the singing, praise for the morning,**

> Praise from them springing fresh from the word.
> **We praise with elation, praising this morning**
> **God's recreation of the new day.**
>
> *Eleanor Farjeon, adapted*

> In this familiar place,
> **we know the mystery of your grace**

> Within this narrow sphere,
> **we learn that you are everywhere.**
>
> *Adapted from a hymn by Colin Gibson*

Where mountains rise to open skies,
**your name, O God is echoed far.**

Where mountains rise to open skies,
**may your way of peace distil the air,**
**your spirit bind all humankind,**
**one covenant of life to share.**

*Adapted from a hymn by Shirley Erena Murray*

# Prayers of Approach

*Approach 1*

Blessed God, we come to this place
To be put in touch with your Spirit.
**We seek to sharpen our awareness**
**of your presence with us.**

Surprising God,
You meet us in ways we do not expect.
We ask for success,
**You teach us acceptance.**

We ask to be loved,
**You ask us to love**

We ask for ease,
**You challenge us.**

We ask for certainty,
**You fill us with questions.**

We expect to find you in piety,
**And discover you can be found anywhere.**

We expect you to use the best people,
**Yet you often use the most unlikely folk**

We are glad of this God,
**Because our hope is that you will use us. Amen.**

*Approach 2*

The God of all generations gathers us
to celebrate our common heritage in Jesus Christ.
**On this particular Sunday we will explore
our identity as Christians mindful of ___.**
[peace, poverty, inequality, families, science...]

The Loving Spirit longs to transform us,
not through nostalgia, but through new awareness.
**Enriched by the past and open to new insights,
we seek to praise God in ways right for our time.**

As truth is newly perceived by each generation,
**we gather now, here, to worship the living God. Amen.**

*Approach 3*

From sandy beach to mountains reach,
**We see your attention to detail
and know you care about
small as well as large.**

We look to you for guidance,
We look to you for comfort,
**We look to you for strength,
We look to you for calm and peace.**

In the midst of our lives –
busy lives, and quiet lives
**You are the one who finds us –
even when we are not searching.**

You meet us with blessings
of hope and encouragement.
**You come through beauty, joy, and sorrow,
sharing the love and goodness that is yourself.**

You come through words we read and people we meet.
**In this time of prayer make us able to receive;**

In this time of searching may what is sought be found;
**In this time of petition may what is asked be granted.**

Clear our minds and open our hearts to truth,
**truth about ourselves, one another, and you;**

Fill our hearts and open our lives to love,
**as we commit to following the example of Jesus. Amen.**

## Approach 4

God of blessings,
**We are thankful that we are not alone,**
**that we have been placed in community.**

We are thankful that we live in your world;
**A world skewed towards good and not evil;**

a world which rates compassion
higher than complacency;
**a world where love is cherished and**
**creatively expressed.**

Confront and stir us from dullness of perception;
forgive our lack of response to your Spirit.
**Sharpen our awareness of holy ground;**
**Prompt us to turn aside and see wonders.**

Forgive us if we have made your world less loving
and help us live life as your daughters and sons,
actively engaged in life's wonders and concerns.
**Forgive us for times when we have over-reacted,**
**and for times when we have lagged in zeal.**

Encourage us to speak the truth we know
and to act in love wherever love is needed.
**Enable us to live in your strength and power,**
**liberated for the possibilities of the future. Amen.**

*Approach 5*

We meet here this morning
**aware there is so much**
**we do not know about you;**

and on reflection,
much we do not know about
those who meet here with us.
**Forgive our lack of interest**
**and our lack of understanding.**

Some of us can't fit in all we need to do;
For others of us time hangs heavy.
We all have issues be it lack of time
or lack of health and energy.

**Whatever we lack,**
**we can all have fellowship,**

for we come as followers of Christ,
**with the hope of knowing more of you,**
**and becoming more caring of each other;**
**Help us worship you in spirit and truth. Amen.**

*Approach 6*

(Adapted from a prayer in 'An old Prayer Book')

There is more light than shadow;
**more grass grows on the meadow.**

There is more song than weeping;
**There is more golden reaping.**

There is more peace than terror;
**There is more truth than error.**

Life is full of guessings,
**But when mindful of life's blessings,**

there are more smiles than cares;
**than brambles, weeds, and tares.**

There is more sun than rain;
**than lost and blighted grain.**

There is more hope than fear;
**more rights than wrongs appear.**

No matter what we do –
**our souls want to worship you. Amen.**

## Prayers before the Reflection / Sermon

*Before the reflection 1*
May the words of my mouth
And the meditations of our hearts
Be acceptable to you O God,
our strength and our redeemer. Amen.

*Psalm 19:14*

*Before the reflection 2*
Spirit of Life,
As we struggle to understand your Holy Word,
Open our minds to exciting possibilities;
Free us to respond to the power of story,
Teach us, delight us, and move us on;
For your song is true,
Your voice is love.
May your holy words power us to holy thinking
and open us to engaging with you. Amen.

*Before the reflection 3*
There are many things
that we do not understand.
Your plan is draped in mystery.
It is not our destiny to know all,
But it is your gift for us to feel, to sense and wonder.
Our essence is sustained by story and ritual,
nurture and nature.
Quicken our senses to glimpse the divine
in unexpected places,
so we are continually surprised by joy. Amen.

## Offertory / Offering Prayers

### Offering 1

God of all, we know these offerings
are part of your creation,
And like us, money and possessions can be used to
achieve good and ill.
We pray that the offerings passing through this parish
will be used wisely,
With our money we offer ourselves
to be used in your service. Amen.

### Offering 2

In this act we identify with the cause of Christ;
**As people of God we offer what we have.**

We proclaim our concern for all people;
**In offering ourselves, money, time and effort,**
**We bring Christ into this moment of history. Amen.**

### Offering 3

Parent God, help us to know the truth
of your love in our lives;
Enable us to grow in the wisdom we need
to be agents of change for a better world.
**We dedicate ourselves and our gifts to your service.**
**Amen.**

### Offering 4

God we are grateful that we know some of your stories
**Help us to use this knowledge wisely.**

Because we have understanding
of what you require of us,
**We ask that you bless the money we bring,**
**May it be used to further your Kingdom. Amen.**

*Offering 5*

Gracious God we ask your blessing
on ourselves and what we give.
**Help us use our money and our talents well.**
**May our gifts encourage generous living**
**and abundant life. Amen.**

*Offering 6*

God, we understand this ritual offering as a symbol,
**Our cash and cheques confirm our commitment;**

Bless this offering of our automatic payments
and our random giving.
**Our pledge is to honour you in all areas of our lives,**
**Help us to honour what we pledge. Amen.**

*Offering 7*

Creating God,
**We pledge commitment to your continuing goodness**

Some of us have more resources than others
**But we bring what we are able**

Bless what we bring
**Our money, our abilities, ourselves,**

That all may be used in creating more goodness
**For our church, our community, and our world,**
**Keep us mindful all of these are loved by you. Amen**

*Offering 8*

God of all,
**bless all of us;**
**Bless how we give,**
**Bless what we give,**
**May all be used well in your service. Amen.**

*Offering 9*

As citizens of this world,
**We commit to living responsibly;**

As parishioners of this parish,
**We commit to this faith community.**

Responsibility and commitment cost,
**A cost of time and a cost of money.**

Bless what we give and may all be used
**in the spirit of commitment and responsibility. Amen.**

*Offering 10*
(from a hymn)

> **We give Thee but Thine own,**
> **Whate'er the gift may be;**
> **All that we have is Thine alone,**
> **A trust, O Lord, from Thee. Amen.**

# Pastoral Prayers / Intercessions

*Pastoral Prayers 1*
Loving God,
We live in community – local, national, and international.
We bring before you concerns that weigh on our hearts
In silence we name before you, world issues…
In silence we name before you, national issues…
In silence we name before you, local issues…
In silence we remember before you
the people of this parish…
In silence we name before you,
people who are loved by us…
Hold them in your love for us.

God of grieving we would bow with you in mourning;
God of suffering we would sit with you in silence;
God of purpose we would stand with you
in determination;
God of journeys we would walk beside you:
We would be your people and do your tasks.
Show us how Lord.
We ask in your name. Amen.

## Pastoral Prayers 2

Immortal, Invisible, God only Wise,
**Immortal God, in you we trust;**
**We give thanks for the eternal assurance of faith.**

We come from a long tradition
of those who seek you in the community of Church.
We meet now in this place
seeking to enrich our faith through worship.
**We seek release from all that hinders us from**
**encountering you.**

*Invisible* God, in you we trust;
**we give thanks for the intangibles**
**that confirm your reality –**

the comfort of love; the ability to trust;
the hope that faith keeps resurrecting,
and the inclination to goodness
you seeded in humankind.
**Enable us to use our faith**
**to do justice and love kindness.**

*Wise* God, in you we trust;
**we give thanks that you are there when we understand,**

and you are there when we don't understand.
As we live within you, may you live within us.
**Grant us the wisdom to walk**
**in humble confidence with you.**

God of *justice, kindness* and *mercy,*
**May we never forget that we are made in your image,**

Grant us a vibrant faith
that increasingly reflects the Way of Christ.
**We come in faith.**
**We come seeking to be better people. Amen.**

### *Pastoral Prayers 3*

God, whose name is 'Goodness,'
We know we can pray to you at any time and in any place,
But this time is special to this parish in this place.
This is when we as a congregation focus on
the needs special to this parish,
this community, the wider world, and ourselves.
At this time our prayer is not in the isolation of
individual littleness,
At this time our personal prayers gather strength from
the prayers of all present.

We open ourselves to the power of united goodness
and pray in silence for those matters that concern us:

We pray for our world,
people and places far away from this place,
people and places connected to us
by the bond of humanity…

We pray for our community,
the needs of people connected to us
by physical location…

We pray for those close to us through
work place, social commitments, or neighbourhood…

We pray for this parish… and these particular people…

We pray for our families… and we pray for ourselves…

These things we pray in your name. Amen.

# Prayers for Particular Sundays

*Prayer of Approach for a New Year*

A New Year for some stretches clear,
beckoning with opportunities,
For others it looms ominously shadowed,
with limitations and challenge;
But whatever this year brings,
we know you are there God,
understanding all, delighting with us,
sorrowing with us and loving us no matter what.
Regardless how many summers we have seen,
the New Year arrives,
offering fresh hope and renewed faith. Amen.

*Prayer of Petition for a New Year*

God of our yesterdays
and God of our tomorrows,
we ask that you be with us now,
God of our today.

We pause on the brink of a New Year
uncertain and unprepared,
but if you are with us we are unafraid.
We know not what to expect.
Our desire is to be equipped for what is to come.
Our hope is to travel light,
and to carry what is best from the past to the future.

God of Vision and New Possibilities,
open our hearts and minds to the reality
of your presence.
God of Light illuminate the dark places of our lives.
We are not perfect people.
Come through the cracks of our imperfections
and fill us with your light.

We pray for all marginalised people.
Those who suffer discrimination because of:
gender, sexual orientation, race, impairment, or creed.
Give them strength and belief in their worth.

We pray for those active in discrimination,
and for those who allow it to happen.
May they know what they do.
May they understand the hurts they cause.

We gather our thoughts in this sacred place,
Knowing that you have heard each sincere desire.
We long for a time when all people are valued.
May our unconditional love flow from us to others,
May it swirl and curl through the year,
embracing all who seek a better life. Amen.

### Children's Day (1st Sunday in March)

### Prayer for Children

God, we come to you with confidence,
Knowing Jesus claimed you as a loving parent.
Though divinity is beyond our comprehension,
Parenting is within our understanding;
We pause to give thanks for our human parents.

Though life is layered with complexity,
Childhood is within our understanding,
We pause to give thanks for our own childhood…

Today we particularly remember today's children,
We ask that those who care for them may do it well;
As participants or onlookers keep us mindful,
That it takes a community to raise a child.

We think of particular children and ask your blessing;
Children known to us by family connection…
Children of our neighbourhood…
Children of this church…
Other Children whose lives intersect with ours…
Children known to us through news media…

However, the little ones are known to us,
We know you know each and every one,
And neither life nor death
can separate them from you. Amen.

### A Child's bed-time prayer

Now I lay me down to sleep,
I pray the Lord my soul will keep.
Be with me through the dark of night,
And when I wake to morning's light.
Bless all the people who love me dear,
May I to them show the same care. Amen.

*Traditional adapted*

[A good prayer to teach the whole congregation as it
connects with grandparents. Some in my congregation
taught it to their grandchildren.]

### Harvest

Abundant God,
this Sunday we particularly remember the harvest
and your enduring goodness to us.
As crops mature and trees fruit
we are surrounded by autumn blessings.
We give thanks for the bounty of the soil.

Because your creativity is infinite,
we are able to appreciate an amazing variety of food.
We offer thanks for your plenitude and our abundance.

Though grateful for farms, orchards and gardens,
ours is not primarily an agricultural environment,
and we have thanks to give for many blessings.

We give thanks for employment.
Some of us are grateful for continuing employment,
and some for employment past.
For the benefits of work, we thank you.
In these uncertain times we pray for those
whose continuing employment is uncertain,
and for those who have been made redundant.
Give them courage, and hope.
Give wisdom and compassion to those
who are able to influence national and global economies.

We give thanks for leisure.
We are grateful for the natural beauty of Aotearoa,
and the opportunities we have
to enjoy so many good things.

We give thanks for the people of this church,
and the many fine companions we
encounter as we travel with you.
Help us to find goodness and God
in all whom we meet, and wherever we go.

Save us from becoming cynics.
Help us to be blessing counters all the days of our lives,
dwelling mindful of your continuing love,
now and forever. Amen.

## Palm Sunday

The festival of Palm Sunday is a Christian custom,
a custom that extends back almost to the year dot.
Each succeeding year the faithful give voice to hope,
not merely in devout song, but in cheers of acclamation.
Waving greenery wafts whispers of liberation,
– whispers that rise to crescendos of joy.

On reflection, the commemoration is peculiar...
Because we know what that first crowd didn't know,
We know how the journey ended...
So why add our hosannas to theirs?

Is it because a divine spark resides in all humans,
a spark that calls us to rejoice in the journey,
a spark that says no matter how it ends
life is more about the journey than the destination.
What can be celebrated should be celebrated,
Hope and joy last beyond death. Amen.

## Palm Sunday - *prayer of approach*

O God, like the people of ancient Jerusalem,
We are hungry for a hero
and crave a glimpse of greatness.

**We gather religiously but lack the passion
of those who watched that long-ago parade.**

That company of ordinary folk jostled
with anticipation hoping to glimpse the Messiah.

We lack their deep hope for a better world;
We are not given to wild impulsive worship;

**We do not see grandeur in the mundane,
or the possibility of a peasant becoming a king.**

We are dull and predictable people,
who attend weekly worship by habit.
**Forgive our lack of hope and fervour, and our
unwillingness to see good or God in unlikely places.**

We ask for the ability to hope with joyful anticipation,
and for willingness to risk being part of the action;
to be open to the potential of life changing events;
and determined do our bit to bring it about.

**We like to think Lord, that we would not have only
waved palms and shed cloaks, but we would have
stayed by the cross, visited the tomb,
and kept belief in love alive.**

We pledge to continue your mission;
to be your people,
in good times and in bad.
**May darkness not overcome us,
may the fullness of love surround us,
enabling us to abide in God,
henceforth and evermore. Amen.**

*Palm Sunday Offertory*

Surprising God,
**Open our eyes to behold the wonder
of your mighty acts.**

You free our beings to proclaim the good news.

**Our hearts sing 'Hosanna in the highest'
for Christ has entered our lives.**

**Accept these offerings as our garlands of welcome,
and our deeds as silent shouts of praise. Amen.**

*Palm Sunday / Easter Commission*

Go with hosannas in your hearts;
Go out into the world in peace;
Go reminded that love triumphs over evil.

**We are free to live and die with courage,
trusting in God, our strength,
Jesus our example,
and the Holy Spirit, our support.**

*Prayer of Approach for Eastertide*

Eternal God,
you have come to us through Jesus crucified;
**We come to you as Easter People,
your sons and daughters, alive with his life,
asking for his power to make us witnesses
of your love at work in the world.**

We thank you for the role model men and women,
Who through the ages have been nourished
by the love of Christ
and have shared what was given them.
Through them we still hear the word
and receive your power.

**We thank you that we are able to share with each other:
friendship and fellowship; joys and sorrows;
service to others and worship together.**

Loving Parent, we have not seen our brother Jesus
with our own eyes,
Nor have we touched his body with our hands,
but we believe in him.

**Fill us with your Holy Spirit,**
**So we can live our lives as he exampled.**
**Bless us as we seek personal understanding,**
**of what it means to be your daughters and sons. Amen.**

*Easter Meditation: The Work of Easter*
> *With thanks to Thurman, Tirabassi, and Strathdee*

(May fit *Light of the world* without chorus: With One Voice 669)

When the song of the wind starts to growl,
when the clouds dim the sun in the sky,
when the chocolate eggs are melted,
and bunnies back to being pests,
the work of Easter has begun:

To show the stricken that we care,
to ease their heavy load of loss,
to call on shut-ins often,
with warmth and good cheer,
and share the now, that is their long goodbye.

When winter prods and Easter prompts us:
We can write to friends not on the net,
and stand against oppression,
and notice the wronged,
and send submissions to those who the hold power.

When winter prods and Easter prompts us:
Let's move from cosy indoor comfort,
turn thought into action,
don't delay to see Christ alive
in the peace where we can pass it, in deed.

### *Prayer for ANZAC Day*
(Nearest Sunday to 25 April)

Today we come mindful of the futility of war...
the suffering, pain, and destruction it inflicts;
The waste and trauma,
and long shadows it casts
down the generations.

We pray that humankind
will evolve beyond this
primitive concept of violence
being a solution.

Despite our physical distance from
the current atrocities of war
we hold war memories,
personal, or passed to us.
We pray for family members
whose lives were terminated
or blighted by war...

Despite our physical distance from
hideous actions delivered
under tags of retribution,
rights, and justice,
graphic images bombard us
planted by ever present
'breaking news' camera angles.
We pray for all who suffer in today's conflicts...

We pray for those who hold power
and treat people as pawns.
May they know what they do
and be motivated to cease from evil

and find solutions in compassion,
mutual respect, and true liberty for all. Amen.

***Prayer for Mothering Sunday / Mothers' Day / Home and Family Sunday***
(Second Sunday in May)

Love-maker, Pain-bearer, Father and Mother of us all,
We know that no matter what we do you keep loving us,
**Help us to justify your love by living loving lives.**

On this Home and Family Sunday,
we give special thanks for families.
From our earliest days we had relations to call our own,
**We thank you that we were born into a family.**

Bless all families – nuclear families, single-parent families,
separated families, inter-generational families,
blended families, chosen families, foster families…
**Whatever its composition, may each family be a unit of love.**

We pray also for the extended family –
grandparents, uncles, aunts,
nephews, nieces, cousins, step-children
and God-children.
**Enable each to play their part and know the joy of connectedness.**

Bless all adults who interact with
children and young people,
May they enjoy this responsibility and
mentor with wisdom and patience,
**Equip and re-equip each of us
for our ever-changing society.**

We give thanks for fathers and
the particular parenting they bring.
We give thanks for mothers and
the particular parenting they bring.
**Help all parents fulfil their roles
with competency and joy.**

As our country celebrates Mothers' Day
we give special thanks for mothers.

Thank you for creating the concept of motherhood and
the gift of mothering.
**Enable all motherly women to put their mothering
skills to good purpose.**

Help us to carry and share the best things we learned
from our mothers.
In silence we name our mothers and
their virtues before you...
**We think of our own mothers and offer our thanks.**

Bless each mother represented here,
wherever she may be.
**Bless us, the children of mothers,
and the children of you,
May we be worthy of the relationship. Amen.**

## Winter

Winters come seasonally, and personally;
chills and darkness that make us yearn
for days that have gone.

Yet, you God, created a cycle of seasons:
Spring's expectation,
Summer's vigour,
Autumn's fruition, and
Winter's contemplation.

In the cold of winter nature takes stock,
unwinds, rests, waits until the time is right.
The endless cycle of seasons
is a model for lives
showing how each season contributes to the whole.

We thank you God for the winters in our lives,
for without cold we could not appreciate warmth,
and without discomfort we may not take time to reflect
upon the width and depth of life,
and the faith in which we live,
or number the blessings that we have.

Help us find spirituality in winter's patterns,
to see beauty in its bareness
and promptings to unclutter our souls and our lives.

We give thanks for the comforts of winter:
that cosiness that exists only in the midst of cold,
for hearty food, wrapping warm, and focussed heat,
for extra indoor time offering more leisure hours,
for books, hobbies, and companionship.
Help us to use our winters to invest hope
in days yet to be. Amen.

### Prayers for Disability Sunday
(Third Sunday in June)

God of struggles, strengths, and strategies,
help us to cope with what we have.

God of difficulties, disabilities, and delights,
help us find joy in who we are.

God of individuality and invisibilities,
enable us to understand how life is harder
for some than it is for their peers;
Give us a readiness to ease difficulties,
remove barriers, and
create level playing fields.

Bless us with the will to appreciate
the courage, creativity, and skills
required to live with impairment;
along with the discernment to realise
impairment is merely a fragment
of personhood.

Empower us all to live in fullness,
valuing what we have,
and knowing we are loved.

At this time we direct our thoughts
and prayers towards those who
suffer life-blighting hidden disabilities;

And, we think of those who are:
Crippled by accident or illness;
Deaf to the sound of voice and music;
Blind to the beauty of form and colour;
Rendered mute by malformation or disaster,
and those disabled by frailty or malfunction.
May they experience the love and care they need,
and may we be instrumental in loosening
the shackles of their dis-ease.

We pray also for those who are:
Blighted by ego;
Crippled by fears;
Deaf to pleadings;
Blind to injustices;
Rendered mute by apathy;
and disabled by bitterness.
May they experience the love and care they need,
and may we be instrumental in loosening
the shackles of their dis-ease. Amen.

• • •

Loving God,
We acknowledge that regardless of health,
attitude, appearance or status,
we are people marred by imperfections.
Grant us the strength to manage our infirmities
with wise caring, good humour, and gratitude.
Help us use whatever we have to become
more insightful to the conditions of humans,
and more attentive to matters spiritual.
Save us from falling victim to self-centredness
– a malaise that preys on the fit and the unfit,
that left unchecked is more soul destroying,
and more binding than any physical aberration.
In the loving of others may we find perfection. Amen.

*Father's Day*
(First Sunday in September)

Loving God,
This Fathers' Day we give thanks for our human fathers,
and pray your blessing on the fathers,
grandfathers and uncles,
in this church, and in our community.
Help them to be good role models
for all the children they encounter.
We know that some in our country do not have
the love and stability of a good father,
So today we pray for special care of the fatherless.
We ask you to bless and strengthen all separated parents,
help them to find the support they need,
to enable good family values in difficult circumstances.
We thank and praise you that we can know you
as God and Father,
through Jesus, our brother in Christ. Amen.

**World Communion**
(First Sunday in October)

On this World Communion Sunday,
We think of people all round the world.
We come before you mindful of our commonality,
Help us retain the virtues shared by all cultures
and all religions.
Give us the will to accept difference,
And help us to unite in the essentials.

Even within our own communities,
We find communication difficult
Show us how to be in communion
with those who do not see as we see.
Help us to understand
what shapes individuals and nations.
Give us the desire to ever seek justice,
And live as a community that rejoices in diversity.

And now we bring our particular concerns before you…

As we face life, O God,
sing to us your song of encouragement,
paint for us your pictures of a new world
where all people live as citizens,
treated with respect and equality,
where no one lacks love or understanding,
and justice is a shared commonality.
Help us to live as part of your new creation.
We pray in the name of Jesus the Christ. Amen.

## *Labour Day 25th October*
(Nearest Sunday)

God of Nations, we are proud of ours and give thanks
that we live in this country.
We are proud to own a founding document,
conceived in a time of peace.
Most treaties are the result of war,
but Our Treaty offers the hope of covenant.
We give thanks that we live in a place of peace and
good intention.

We know human rights do not simply happen,
they are initiated by people of vision,
Negotiated by people wanting justice,
and often achieved at considerable cost.
We give thanks for our forebears who worked for justice.

Despite our proud record of justice and
good working conditions,
Some of our citizens are exploited,
disadvantaged and dis-empowered,
Be with those who are working for justice now.

Despite our fine laws on human rights,
some of our citizens continue to be discriminated against,
through circumstances of education, employment, race,
disability, gender, and sexual orientation.

We pray for those who are over-worked,
and those who are unemployed.
We pray for the ill-treated, the un-treated,
the dis-empowered and the ignored.

We pray for all who oppress,
be they deliberately malicious or merely insensitive,
bosses or bullies, law-makers or church-people;
may they be confronted by their actions
and moved to bring change.
May wisdom prevail.

We pray for families,
in all their diversities,
whatever form they take,
that love may prevail. Amen.

### Labour Day (with responses)
Eternal God,
For the privilege of living in New Zealand:
**We give you thanks.**

For the abundance of good things that surround us –
natural beauty, clean air and good food:
**We give you thanks.**

We are proud to own a founding document
conceived in a time of peace.
Most treaties are the result of war but,
Our Treaty offers the hope of covenant.
**We give thanks that we live in a place of peace and
good intention.**

We live in a country that: deplores racism;
enshrines human rights in law;
where all citizens regardless of religion,
race or nationality may live as equals.
**We are grateful, and we offer our thanks.**

Human rights do not simply happen,
they are initiated by people of vision,

negotiated by people wanting justice,
and achieved at considerable cost.
**We give thanks for our forebears
who worked for justice.**

Despite our proud record of justice
and good working conditions
Some of our citizens are exploited, disadvantaged
and dis-empowered,
**Be with those who are working for justice now.**

In this land of equal opportunity,
certain groups experience discrimination,
**We pray for that we may never contribute to
discrimination.**

Some of our people allow anger and discontent
to disrupt into violence.
We pray that anger and discontent be channelled
into positive action.
Enable those with power to listen with care;
Grant them the wisdom and vision
to share this land's resources with fairness and justice.
**Be with us as we here meet in your name.**

We give thanks for the many individuals
who take up the tasks of this place,
those who enable it to function,
those who give this church its character.
**May each of us have reason to know
we are a blessed member
of this particular Church Family. Amen.**

### Reign of Christ the King
(November: last Sunday of Liturgical Year)

Loving God,
As living pace quickens towards our end of year,
help us respond with spiritual energy,
energy gathered from the cycle of the year past.

In our Christian calendar this day marks
the culmination of the Liturgical Year.

We have lived the journey from:
out of wedlock, out of town,
out of shelter and on-the-run;

To growing in wisdom and stature;
baptism, temptations, gathering disciples,
preaching, teaching, stories and healings,
persecution and death, to resurrection and glory.

Lessen our desire to cling to facts,
free us to embrace the deep spirituality
of mythical journey that culminates in kingship.
Kingship equates to mastery, strength, wealth and power.
Help us understand the mysterious ways
of Divine Kingship.

May we dwell on the inspiration of your Kingdom,
a Kingdom of kindness and justice, health and wholeness,
the Kingdom of Christ where all are valued.
To dwell on your Kingdom brings invitation,
to dwell in your Kingdom.
Because your Kingdom is within us,
Help us make your Kingdom come. Amen.

### December: Advent

Help us live this Advent,
mindful of the true meaning of Christmas.
As we contemplate the birth of a special child,
Keep us aware that each of us is a special child of yours.
The Christ Child heralded a new way of being;
A way that replaces rules with values,
darkness with hope,
tumult with peace,
sadness with joy,
and love at the heart of all. Amen.

### Advent offertory

We gratefully accept your gifts
of hope, love, joy and peace;
Help us give them to others;
Bless this offering,
as a tangible token of our intent. Amen.

### Advent Benediction

Let us not KEEP Christmas.
Let us GIVE Christmas.
Let us LIVE Christmas – merrily, responsibly,
With sparkling eyes, till it comes again.

# Benedictions / Commissions

### Commission 1

Our God is a God of covenant,
**We are partners in the work of salvation.**
**May the gospel be confirmed in us,**
**as we seek the excellence to which God calls us.**

### Commission 2

Live as Easter people,
Live with celebration,
Live with joy and hope.
**We are an Easter People,**
**We commit to following the Jesus Way.**

### Commission 3

Go as members of this church,
to do the work of God in this community.
**We go as Christian citizens,**
**to do the work of God in this land.**

Go as individuals and go as one people.
**We go rejoicing in our diversity**
**and delighting in our companions.**

## Commission 4

Be confident that God is good, and love is of God.
Be confident that God is in you and you are in God.
Be confident that there is good and God in everyone.
Go confident in the power of the Holy Spirit.
**We go to reflect goodness and love,**
**We go to live confident Godly lives.**

## Commission 5

Go with your strength renewed in God.
**We go confident that you are a good God,**
**We go confident that you are a loving God.**

Go invigorated by the power of the Holy Spirit,
Go to reflect love and goodness in all you do.
**We commit to following the loving example of Jesus.**

## Commission 6

Blessings abound, accept the bounty;
Be empowered by Scripture and story.
Know God speaks through Scripture,
Know God speaks through story,
Know God is in your story,
Know God speaks through you.

## Commission 7

Depart in peace;
**We go to love.**

Go rejoicing in difference;
**We go to hear.**

Go assured God is with us,
**We go to care.**

**Commission 8**

Let us go gladly
as people who commit to Jesus,
**Hosanna in the name of the Lord.**

May our Hosannas translate
into active understanding
of living the Jesus Way,
**Hosanna in the name of the Lord.**

*Commission 9*

**We go from this place with glad hearts;**

Go boldly; go knowing you are loved;
**We go as instruments of God's peace,**

Go as bringers of hope and liberty;
**We will walk as true followers of Jesus Christ.**

*Commission / Affirmation 10*

With your help O God:
**We reject victim mentality;**

Live as survivors;
**We will do the best we can;**

Invest in theology;
**We will be people of faith.**

Go out into the everyday world, where Jesus walked,
learning from the example lived among us:
Go into a world where there are many wildernesses,
Where we may feel undervalued; experience rejection;
be misunderstood, or simply not be noticed.
But Christ is crucified and risen;
And God is good.

**We meet the cross and reach for resurrection life;**
**Our greatest joy is found in doing God's will. Amen.**

## Famous Prayers

### The Aaronic Blessing
(Possibly the oldest prayer we use frequently.
Now we usually say 'you' instead of 'thee.')

> The Lord bless thee and keep thee:
> The Lord make his face shine upon thee,
> and be gracious unto thee:
> The Lord lift up his countenance upon thee,
> and give thee peace.

*Numbers 6:24–26, KJV*

### The Lord's Prayer
> Our Father which art in heaven,
> Hallowed be thy name.
> Thy kingdom come,
> Thy will be done in earth,
> as it is in heaven.
> Give us this day our daily bread.
> And forgive us our debts,
> as we forgive our debtors.
> And lead us not into temptation,
> but deliver us from evil:
> For thine is the kingdom,
> and the power, and the glory,
> now and forever. Amen.

*Matthew 6:9–13, KJV*

### The Grace
> The grace of our Lord Jesus Christ,
> The love of God,
> And the fellowship of the Holy Spirit
> be with us all. Amen

*2 Corinthians 13:14*

> Most High, Glorious God,
> enlighten the darkness of our minds.
> Give us a right faith, a firm hope and a perfect charity,

so that we may always and in all things
act according to Your Holy Will. Amen.

*St Francis of Assisi, 1181–1226*

## Peace

Lord, make me an instrument of your peace.
Where there is hatred, let me sow love,
Where there is injury, pardon
Where there is doubt, faith,
Where there is despair, hope,
Where there is darkness, light,
Where there is sadness, joy.

O Divine Master, grant that I may not so much
seek to be consoled as to console,
not so much to be understood as to understand,
not so much to be loved, as to love;
for it is in giving that we receive,
it is in pardoning that we are pardoned,
it is in dying that we awake to eternal life. Amen.

*St. Francis of Assisi, 1181–1226*

## Day by Day

Thanks be to thee, Lord Jesus Christ,
for all the benefits which thou hast won for us,
for all the pains and insults which thou hast borne for us.
O most merciful Redeemer, Friend and brother,
may we know thee more clearly, love thee more dearly,
and follow thee more nearly, day by day. Amen.

*Richard of Chichester, 1197–1253*

God, of your goodness, give me yourself;
for you are sufficient for me.
I cannot properly ask anything less, to be worthy of you.
If I were to ask less, I should always be in want.
In you alone do I have all. Amen.

*Julian of Norwich, b. 1342*

Teach us, Lord,
To serve you as you deserve,
To give and not to count the cost,
To fight and not to heed the wounds,
To toil and not to seek for any reward,
Save that of knowing that we do your will. Amen.

*Ignatius Loyola, 1491–1556*

From silly devotions and from sour-faced saints,
Good Lord, deliver us.

Let nothing disturb you; let nothing dismay you;
All things pass: God never changes.
Patience attains all it strives for.
Those who have God find they lack nothing:
God suffices.

Christ has no body now on earth but yours;
Yours are the only hands with which he can do his work,
Yours are the only feet with which he can
go about the world,
Yours are the only eyes through which his compassion
can shine forth upon a troubled world.

*St Teresa of Avila, 1515–1582*

God be in my head and in my understanding;
God be in my eyes and in my looking;
God be in my mouth and in my speaking;
God be in my heart and in my thinking;
God be at my end and at my departing. Amen.

*Sarum [Salisbury] Primer Prayer, 1588*

O Lord, help me not to despise or oppose
what I do not understand. Amen.

*William Penn [Quaker], 1644-1718*

### A Daily Prayer

Morning and evening
I commit my soul to Jesus Christ,
the saviour of the world.
Enable me, O God, to observe what he saith unto me:
resolutely to obey his precepts
and endeavour to follow his example
in those things wherein he is exhibited to us
as a pattern for our imitation.
Make plain to me that circumstance
not time of life can occur
but I may find something either
spoken by our Lord Himself or
by His Spirit in the prophets or
apostles that will direct my conduct
if I am but faithful to thee and my own soul. Amen.

*Susanna Wesley, 1669–1742*

### The Covenant Prayer

I am no longer my own, but yours,
Put me to what you will, rank me with whom you will;
Put me to doing, put me to suffering;
Let me be employed for you, or laid aside for you,
Exalted for you or brought low for you.
Let me be full, let me be empty;
Let me have everything, let me have nothing.
I freely and with all my heart,
Yield everything to your pleasure and disposal.
And now blessed Lord God,
Creator, redeemer, Holy Spirit,
I am yours, and you are mine.
So be it.
And the covenant which I have made on earth,
Let it be ratified in heaven. Amen.

*John Wesley, 1703–1791*

### Forgiveness

Forgive them all, O Lord;
Our sins of omission and our sins of commission;
The sins of our youth and the sins of our riper years;
The sins of our souls and the sins of our bodies;
Our secret and our more open sins;
Our sins of ignorance and surprise,
And our more deliberate and presumptuous sin;
The sins we have done to please ourselves,
And the sins we have done to please others;
The sins we know and remember,
And the sins we have forgotten;
The sins we have striven to hide from others,
And the sins by which we have made others offend;
Forgive them, O Lord, forgive them all for his sake,
Who died for our sins and rose for our justification,
And now stands at thy right hand,
To make intercession for us,
Jesus Christ our Lord.

*John Wesley, 1703–1791*

### Peace

May today there be peace within.
May you trust God that you are
exactly where you are meant to be.
May you not forget the infinite possibilities
that are born of faith.
May you use those gifts that you have received,
and pass on the love that has been given to you.
May you be content knowing you are a child of God.
Let this presence settle into your bones,
and allow your soul
the freedom to sing, dance, praise and love.
It is there for each and every one of us. Amen.

*St Theresa ['of the roses'] Lisieux, 1873–1897*

*Saint Theresa's Prayer (corporate)*
May today there be peace within.
**May we trust God that we are**
**exactly where we are meant to be.**

May we not forget the infinite possibilities
that are born of faith.
**May we use those gifts that we have received,**
**and pass on the love that has been given to us.**

May we be content knowing we are children of God.
**Let this presence settle into our bones,**
**and allow our souls**
**the freedom to sing, dance, praise and love.**

It is there for each and every one of us. Amen.

*Christ has no hands but our hands*
Christ has no hands but our hands, to do His work today,
He has no feet but our feet to lead men in His way.
He has no tongue but our tongue to tell men how He died,
He has no help but our help to bring them to His side.

We are the only Bible, the careless world will read,
We are the sinners' gospel, we are the scoffers' creed.
We are the Lord's last message, given in deed and word,
What if the type is crooked, what if the print is blurred?
What if our hands are busy, with other work than His,
What if our feet are walking, where sin's allurement is?
What if our tongues are speaking,
of things His lips would spurn,
How can we hope to help Him, and hasten His return?
Amen.

*Annie Johnson Flint, 1862–1932*

### Discernment

O God, grant us the serenity
to accept what cannot be changed,
the courage to change what can be changed,
and the wisdom to know the difference. Amen.

*Reinhold Niebuhr, 1892–1971*

### Interdependence

O God, you have bound us together in this bundle of life;
give us grace to understand
how our lives depend on the courage,
the industry, the honesty and integrity
of our fellow men (beings);
that we may be mindful of their needs,
grateful for their faithfulness,
and faithful in our responsibilities to them;
through Jesus Christ our Lord. Amen.

*Reinhold Niebuhr, 1892–1971*

### Fill us with love

Fill us with love,
and let us be bound together with love
as we go our diverse ways,
united in one spirit
which makes You present in the world.
And which makes you witness to
the ultimate reality that is love.
Love has overcome. Love is victorious. Amen.

*Thomas Merton, 1915–1968*

### The Wire Fence

The wires are holding hands around the holes:
To avoid breaking the ring,
they hold tight the neighbouring wrist,
And it is thus that the holes they make a fence,

Lord, there are lots of holes in my life.
There are some in the lives of my neighbours.

But if you wish we shall hold hands,
We shall hold very tight,
And together we shall make a fine roll of fence,
To adorn Paradise. Amen.

*Michel Quoist, 1918–1997*

### General Confession
Almighty, and most merciful Father;
We have erred, and strayed from thy ways like lost sheep.
We have followed too much the devices and desires
of our own hearts.
We have offended against thy holy laws.
We have left undone those things
which we ought to have done;
And we have done those things
which we ought not to have done;
And there is no health in us.

But thou, O Lord, have mercy upon us,
miserable offenders.
Spare thou those, O God, who confess their faults.
Restore thou those who are penitent;
According to thy promises declared unto mankind
In Christ Jesus our Lord.
And grant, O most merciful Father, for his sake;
that we may hereafter live a godly, righteous,
and sober life,
To the glory of thy holy Name. Amen.

*Book of Common Prayer, 1928*

# Indigenous Blessings
Kia hora te marino, kia whakapapa pounamu te moana,
Kia tere kārohirohi i mua i tou huarahi.

May calm be spread around you,
may the sea glisten like greenstone
and the shimmer of summer dance across your path.

*Māori Blessing*

Go with us Lord wherever we walk;
And speak with us whenever we talk.
Please help us Lord to do as you do,
And through each day be more like you.

*A New Zealand Blessing*

May the road rise up to meet you,
May the wind be ever at your back.
May the sun shine warm upon your face,
And the rain fall softly on your fields.
And until we meet again,
May God hold you in the hollow of his hand.

*Irish Blessing*

## Deep Peace

Deep Peace of the running wave to you;
Deep Peace of the flowing air to you;
Deep Peace of the quiet earth to you;
Deep Peace of the shining stars to you;
Deep Peace of the gentle night to you,
Deep Peace of the Infinite to you.

*(Gaelic Blessing)*

May you have walls for the wind,
a roof for the rain,
and drinks bedside the fire,
Laughter to cheer you and those you love near you,
And all that your heart may desire.

*Celtic Blessing*

May the roof above you never fall in
And may those beneath it never fall out.

*Celtic Blessing*

Oh, Great Spirit, of the Indian *(All)* people,
Hear my words, for they are for you, they are of you.
You are my way of life in the Circle of Life.

*Native American*

### Great Spirit Prayer

Oh, Great Spirit, whose voice I hear in the wind,
whose breath gives life to all the world.
Hear me; I need your strength and wisdom.
Let me walk in beauty,
and make my eyes ever behold the red and purple sunset.
Make my hands respect the things you have made and
my ears sharp to hear your voice make me wise
so that I may understand
the things you have taught my people.
Help me to remain calm and strong
in the face of all that comes towards me.
Let me learn the lessons you have hidden
in every leaf and rock.
Help me seek pure thoughts and
act with the intention of helping others.
Help me find compassion without empathy
overwhelming me.
I seek strength, not to be greater than my brother,
but to fight my greatest enemy – Myself.
Make me always ready to come to you
with clean hands and straight eyes.
So when life fades, as the fading sunset,
my spirit may come to you without shame.

*Native American*

My words are tied in one with the great mountains,
with the great rocks, with the great trees,
in one with my body and heart.
All of you see me, one with this world.

*Yokuts Prayer*

I give you this one thought to keep –
I am with you still – I do not sleep.
I am a thousand winds that blow,
I am the diamond glints on snow,
I am the sunlight on ripened grain,
I am the gentle autumn rain.
When you awaken in the morning's hush,

I am the sweet uplifting rush,
of quiet birds in circled flight.
I am the soft starts that shine at night.
Do not think of me as gone –
I am with you still in each new dawn.

*Native American*

# Other Occasions

## *Before a Service*

Loving God we meet in your name,
Be with all who gather here today;
Free us from the things that may prevent us
From worshipping you;
Prepare our hearts and minds so we may be
refreshed and energised for the continuing journey.
Be with all who contribute to this service,
Grant them what they need to serve you well.
Bless our organist, ushers, stewards and readers,
and those who serve in other ways.
Be with our preacher _____ ,
Give *him / her* sensitivity and understanding,
May *his / her* ordinary words be transformed
to spark and sustain your people.
May this service uplift and challenge,
inform and enliven, and bring us closer to you.
Bless us all, in Jesus name. Amen.

## *Be with us*

Be with us in a special way on this special day
in this special place;
Be with _____ as s/he leads this service
use her / him as your messenger.
Give us listening ears to hear your message and
willing hearts to respond to your message.
We ask your blessing on the organist and reader(s) and
all who contribute to the well-being of this service.
May all leave here as people touched by you.
This we ask in your name. Amen.

### Our Holy Day

This is our Holy Day our Lord
We come to worship you in Spirit and in Truth.
May all who come for comfort, find love;
May all who come from duty, find encouragement;
May all who come seeking, find what they seek.
Support all who lead this service and all who participate.
May we leave knowing we are in your presence. Amen.

### For togetherness

Draw us together, O God,
Into a company of caring disciples;
Unite us as a Christian community;
May we be family
where every member is respected and valued.
May we live valuing difference and rejoicing in diversity
as together we follow the loving example of Jesus. Amen.

### Taken ill in church

Loving God, you know what has happened,
but we are on edge.
We ask for your blessing.
Be with our member (*friend / sister / brother*)
who has so unexpectedly taken ill.
May our love join your love to support __ (*name if
known, otherwise, him / her*)
May _____ be aware of the good intent
that surrounds (*him / her*)
and gain strength of spirit and strength of body.

Be with those who will care for _____.
Guide them to do what is best.
Grant wisdom and patience to the healers and
carers and give _____ your peace that takes away fear.
Calm us so we can resume our worship.
This we ask in the name of Jesus, the great healer. Amen.

### In hospital (unexpectedly)

We are here God and know you are here too.
Help us be aware of your presence. _____ is yours God.
May *(s/he)* take comfort in your presence
knowing you are in this trauma.
Bless those who have medical decisions to make
with the wisdom to do what is most needed.
Restore _____ to the fullness that you can give. Amen.

### Bedside

O Holy Spirit, Giver of Life, Helper and Friend,
Source of all good gifts,
bring peace and comfort to ____.
We give thanks for the skill of surgeons
and the medical benefits that are available here.
Surround _____ with your healing touch.
Bless all who care for _____ grant them what they need
to contribute to the best outcome.
Whatever happens may _____ remain positive
knowing that *(s/he)* is loved by you and
upheld in the loving thoughts of family and friends.
Amen.

### Home Visit

In this moment we ask your blessing on this household.
We give thanks for _____
*(name, this couple, this family).*
May they be aware of your Spirit in this place;
May this household know more joy than pain;
May it be a place of loving relationships
and well-founded happiness;
May problems and fears be worked through
in the light of your love.
Grant those who live here
the knowledge of your blessing. Amen.

### God of journeys

We are vulnerable travellers,
people who carry the baggage of fear and worry.
As we rest in this spot with you we silently name
each fear and worry that we put down...

God who travels each and every journey,
We know that you understand pain and scars;
You know how our journey has wounded us,
As we uncover our wounds in your presence,
We name them silently...

We gratefully accept your healing balm;
Please explain: how it should be applied,
when it should be used, and how frequently...

Did you say seventy times seven?
Isn't that something to do with forgiveness?
Help us forgive ourselves and others,
and bless our baggage with your healing touch.

God of our journeying,
As we continue our journey,
may our loads become easier to carry.
Show us the way to go,
the way to best help those we care about...
and how we can care for this planet that is our home.

God who is our companion,
may we recognise you in our midst,
Live in us as energy and joy,
as our souls reach out to other travellers. Amen.

# 20 — Theology Guides for the 21st Century

## The Millennium Statement

Let there be respect for the earth
Peace for its people
Love in our lives
Delight in the good
Forgiveness for past wrongs
And from now on,
A new start.

*Churches Together' England, 2000*

## The Charter of Compassion

*A universal theology for all preachers*
The principle of compassion lies at the heart of all religious, ethical and spiritual traditions, calling us always to treat all others as we wish to be treated ourselves. Compassion impels us to work tirelessly to alleviate the suffering of our fellow creatures, to dethrone ourselves from the centre of our world and put another there, and to honour the inviolable sanctity of every single human being, treating everybody, without exception, with absolute justice, equity and respect.

It is also necessary in both public and private life to refrain consistently and empathically from inflicting pain. To act or speak violently out of spite, chauvinism, or self-interest, to impoverish, exploit or deny basic rights to anybody, and to incite hatred by denigrating others—even our enemies—is a denial of our common humanity. We acknowledge that we have failed to live compassionately and that some have even increased the sum of human misery in the name of religion.

We therefore call upon all men and women to restore compassion to the centre of morality and religion ~ to

224

return to the ancient principle that any interpretation of scripture that breeds violence, hatred or disdain is illegitimate ~ to ensure that youth are given accurate and respectful information about other traditions, religions and cultures ~ to encourage a positive appreciation of cultural and religious diversity ~ to cultivate an informed empathy with the suffering of all human beings—even those regarded as enemies.

We urgently need to make compassion a clear, luminous and dynamic force in our polarized world. Rooted in a principled determination to transcend selfishness, compassion can break down political, dogmatic, ideological and religious boundaries. Born of our deep interdependence, compassion is essential to human relationships and to a fulfilled humanity. It is the path to enlightenment, and indispensable to the creation of a just economy and a peaceful global community.

*charterforcompassion.org*

### *History*

The Charter for Compassion was conceived by Karen Armstrong, an acclaimed religious scholar and bestselling author. With world-wide support from multi-faith leaders and multi-national thinkers she unveiled the Charter of Compassion in Washington, DC on 12 November 2009. That day, more than 75 launch events took place around the globe and more than 60 Charter for Compassion plaques were hung at significant religious and secular sites around the world.

### *Logo*

The Charter logo incorporates the ancient symbol for infinity. Here used to represent the concept of "endless love" – the limitless potential of compassion to transform human relationships, institutions, and communities through the infinite capacity of human kindness and creativity to relieve suffering, connect us to ourselves and to each other, create justice, heal our planet, and protect the natural world with all its inhabitants.

# 21 — Additional Worship Resources

**Philip Garside** (formerly of Epworth Books) can advise on and supply materials from around the world, that cover all aspects of preparing for worship, including music.

His company is the New Zealand distributor for The New Zealand Hymnbook Trust's music books and CDs, and of the *Seasons of the Spirit* materials produced in Canada. Web: www.pgpl.co.nz  Email: books@pgpl.co.nz Phone: 04 475 8855.

*Word & Worship* the New Zealand lay preachers' magazine available from the **New Zealand Lay Preachers' Association.** Current secretary Nola Stuart. Email: wransnola@xtra.co.nz Web: nzlpa.wordpress.com

**Rev Dr David Bell's** website **Kiwi Connexion**. He offers many printed and visual resources and educational videos, a series of video clips on *The Art and Craft of Shaping a Sermon.* Web: kiwiconnexion.nz

**Methodist Church of NZ** website. Provides ministry / worship resources, particularly useful for preparing services. Includes *10 minutes on Tuesday.* Web: www.methodist.org.nz/resources

## Suggested Books and CDs

These titles can be ordered through Philip Garside Publishing Ltd.

*Christianity / Theology / Commentary*
**Grounded:** *Finding God in the World: A Spiritual Revolution.* Diana Butler Bass. HarperOne (2017).

**What Is the Bible?:** *How an Ancient Library of Poems, Letters, and Stories Can Transform the Way You Think and Feel About Everything.* Rob Bell. HarperOne (2017).

**Days of Awe and Wonder:** *How to Be a Christian in the Twenty-first Century.* Marcus J Borg. HarperOne (2018).

**The Heart of Christianity:** *Rediscovering a Life of Faith.* Marcus J Borg. HarperOne (2004).

**The Power of Parable:** *How Fiction by Jesus Became Fiction About Jesus.* John Dominic Crossan. HarperOne (2013).

**How Jesus Became God:** *The Exaltation of a Jewish Preacher from Galilee.* Bart D Ehrman. HarperOne (2015).

**New World New God:** *Rethinking Christianity for a secular age.* Ian Harris. Makaro Press (2018).

**Short Stories by Jesus:** *The Enigmatic Parables of a Controversial Rabbi.* Amy-Jill Levine. HarperOne (2015).

**Women's Bible Commentary,** 3rd edition. Carol A. Newsom; Sharon H. Ringe eds. Westminster John Knox Press (2015).

**Honest to God** – 40th edition. John A T Robinson. Westminster John Knox Press (1963, 2006).

**The Fourth Gospel:** *Tales of a Jewish Mystic.* John Shelby Spong. HarperOne (2014).

**A Little History of Religion.** Richard Holloway. Yale University Press (2016).

**Paul:** *A Biography.* N T (Tom) Wright. HarperOne (2018).

**The Day the Revolution Began:** *Rethinking The Meaning of Jesus' Crucifixion.* N T (Tom) Wright. HarperOne (2018).

**Simply Good News:** *Why the Gospel Is News and What Makes It Good.* N T (Tom) Wright. HarperOne (2017).

## *Worship / Preaching / Prayers*

**A New Zealand Prayer Book** – Anglican Church in NZ. View full text online at: anglicanprayerbook.nz

**Cloth for the Cradle:** *Worship Resources and Readings for Advent, Christmas and Epiphany.* John L. Bell. Wild Goose Worship Group (1998).

**Gift and Task:** *A Year of Daily Readings and Reflections.* Walter Brueggemann. Westminster John Knox (2017).

**The Canterbury Preacher's Companion:** *150 complete sermons for Sundays, Festivals and Special Occasions.* (Produced for each calendar year). Michael Counsell. Canterbury Press.

**The Zondervan Pastor's Annual:** *An Idea and Resource Book.* (Produced for each calendar year) T T Crabtree. Zondervan.

**Creative Worship Volume 1:** *Songs, Prayers & Poems.* Free PDF eBook. Philip Garside. Philip Garside Publishing Ltd (2017).

**The Abingdon Preaching Annual:** *Planning Sermons and Services for Fifty-Two Sundays* (Produced for each calendar year). Scott Hoezee. Abingdon Press.

**Wild Goose big book of liturgies.** Iona Community. Wild Goose (2017).

**Wild Goose Big Book of Worship Resources.** Iona Community. Wild Goose (2017).

**The Jesus Walk** – PDF eBook. Anna Johnstone. Johnstone2 Photography (2014).

**The Last Walk.** Spiral bound. Anna Johnstone. Johnstone2 Photography (2018).

**Redemption Songs:** *Prayers for people like us.* Mark Laurent. Philip Garside Publishing Ltd (2016).

**Connections:** *A Lectionary Commentary for Preaching and Worship:* (Three volumes for each of lectionary years A, B & C) Thomas G. Long, Cynthia L. Rigby. Luke A. Powery, Joel B. Green. Westminster John Knox (2018).

**All-Age Worship Revised & updated 2nd edition.** Lucy Moore. Bible Reading Fellowship (2016).

**Let Us Pray:** *Intercessions Following The Revised Common Lectionary.* Janet Nelson. HarperCollins (1999).

**The Intercessions Resource Book.** John Pritchard. SPCK. (2018)

**Untamed Gospel:** *Protests, poems and prose for the Christian year.* Martyn Percy; Rowan Williams; Malcolm Guite; Jim Cotter. Canterbury Press (2017).

**The Abingdon Worship Annual:** *Contemporary & Traditional Resources For Worship Leaders.* (Produced for each calendar year). Mary J Scifres; B J Beu. Abingdon Press.

**The Soft Petals of Grace:** *Communion Liturgies and Other Resources.* Thom Shuman. Wild Goose (2016).

**Ten Plays:** *Short, easy dramas for churches.* Rosalie Sugrue. Philip Garside Publishing Ltd (2013).

**Theme Scheme:** *Creative Ideas, Activities, Games, Puzzles, Plays, Quizzes.* Rosalie Sugrue. Philip Garside Publishing Ltd (2014).

**Sophia & Daughters:** *Wise Women from the Bible.* Rosalie Sugrue. Steele Roberts (2014). Now only available as a Kindle eBook from Amazon.com.

**Gifts in Open Hands:** *More Resources from the Global Community.* Maren C. Tirabassi; Kathy Wonson Eddy eds. Pilgrim Press (2011).

**A Child Laughs:** *Prayers of Justice and Hope.* Maren C Tirabassi; Maria Mankin eds. Pilgrim Press (2017).

**Gathering.** Worship planning resource for ministers, lay preachers, music directors and worship teams. Subscription – 4 issues p.a. United Church of Canada. United Church of Canada.

**Will Willimon's Lectionary Sermon Resource:** (2 volumes for each of lectionary years A, B & C) William H Willimon. Abingdon (2018).

*Music books and CDs*
**Hope is Our Song.** Music book (2009) and CD (2010). NZ Hymnbook Trust.

**Carol our Christmas.** Music book (1996) and CD (1996). NZ Hymnbook Trust.

**Faith Forever Singing.** Music book (2000) and CD (2000). NZ Hymnbook Trust.

**Alleluia Aotearoa.** Music book (1989) and CD (1993). NZ Hymnbook Trust.

**Tell My People:** *25 years of Festival Singers.* CD. Festival Singers of Wellington. Festivity Productions (2000).

**Spirited People.** CD. Festival Singers of Wellington. Festivity Productions (2007).

**People of the Light.** Festival Singers of Wellington. CD. Music by Jonathan Berkahn. Festivity Productions (2015).

# Also by Rosalie Sugrue
# Published by Philip Garside Publishing Ltd

 **Ten Plays:** *Short, easy dramas for churches* (**Updated 2018**): Lay preacher Rosalie Sugrue's short plays and meditations are ideal to present in church. They encourage us to engage with Bible and historical characters, and explore important themes. Staging is simple. Few props or costumes are required. (In Print & ebooks)

 **Theme Scheme:** *Creative Ideas, Activities, Games, Puzzles, Plays, Quizzes* (**Updated 2018**): Offers you a wealth of creative ideas, activities, games, puzzles and quizzes to help plan, organise and lead your group's programmes. All are fun and practical, requiring minimal equipment, and time to prepare. (In Print & ebooks)

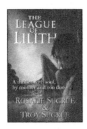 **The League of Lilith:** *A thriller with soul. Written with her son Troy Sugrue* (**2013**): Sarai, a Biblical Studies lecturer, learns a terrible truth; a core knowledge she must impart to a successor. Will she choose society wife, Jen, or bondage and discipline prostitute Kat? An explosive novel with a dramatic climax. (ebooks)

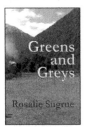 **Greens and Greys (2015):** Journey with Molly Sinclair through her 1950s childhood on the West Coast, her move to Christchurch for teacher training, drama-filled OE in the UK and Europe, and as she returns to NZ in the mid-1960s. An engaging coming-of-age tale. (In Print & ebooks)

 **Green, Ho! (2015):**
*Green, Ho!* is an extended version of *Greens and Greys* that adds another dimension in the form of hidden disability. (In Print & ebooks)

Made in the USA
Middletown, DE
04 June 2021